WITHIN WITHOUT

The Path of the Yogi

By

BRIANA BLASKO

Introduction by Pico Iyer

CONTRIBUTORS

Tsering Palmo Gellek
Ratna Raman
Shyama Warner
Vishnupriya
Justin Peters

HarperCollins *Publishers* India

HarperCollins
PUBLISHERS
Since 1817

First published in India in 2017 by HarperCollins *Publishers*
A-75, Sector 57, Noida, Uttar Pradesh 201301, India
www.harpercollins.co.in

2 4 6 8 10 9 7 5 3 1

ISBN: 978-93-5277-432-6

All of the author's proceeds from the first edition of printing will be donated to the Girl's Education Fund benefitting the Satyachetana Sikhyashram School, Balanga, Odisha.

Book design by Justin Peters

Printed and bound at
Thomson Press (India) Ltd

For my mother,
whose dedication to the path was the seed
of my journey into India.

THE COMMON THREAD

Pico Iyer

India has such a rich and vibrant outer life that it's easy for a visitor to overlook its inner being; so much is going on at every moment, so loudly and with such intensity, often, that one forgets that it's everything before the dance, all the invisible work that precedes any release of action, that gives it soul and direction. The newcomer lost in the Ali Baba exoticism of India's teeming cities can too readily overlook the fact that she's entering a world that gave us a whole practice of contemplation, sometimes called yoga, and the notion of a householder, at a certain stage in life, going off into the wilderness to retrieve a sense of truth.

What moves me in Briana Blasko's quiet, unintrusive photographs – as in her soulful and beautifully lucid Preface – is her readiness to follow India into the silent places where truly its energy lives. You'll notice how many of the people in her work wear white, quite unadorned; you'll register how many of them are Jains, members of the gentle, peace-loving tradition often overlooked in all our clamour over Hindus and Moslems. You'll see how everyday are the places and exchanges she's brought back out into the world, and how these white-clad yogis can carry their sense of stillness and purity into the heart of a noisy city.

When I was a kid, I left my twenty-fifth-floor office in Midtown Manhattan to go to Japan, to live for a year in a temple. My year didn't quite work out as planned, but thirty years on, I'm still near Kyoto, and my life with my wife is often strikingly similar to the simple clarity I longed for on Sixth Avenue. Very soon after I arrived, I was fortunate to meet a Zen master. The whole point of our practice, he told me – he could have been speaking of prayer, of meditation, of yoga, of fasting – lies not in the going away from the world, but in the coming back. The only reason to try to empty yourself out is so that you have more to offer to everyone around you when you step back into the streets.

That's some of the spirit I sense in Briana's collection of offerings, and images of souls alone with their divine. As she says, she took pains not to encroach on people who were going about some of the most intimate moments of their day; often, it seemed best to come away with no images at all. And as she also says, even the images we are lucky enough to view merely point at something that's far less visible, but lived out in eyes and smiles and arms reaching out (to the crowds or to the sun).

Most of all, in a contentious and evermore polarized time, I'm touched at how she finds, in every story she shares here, some universal, human chord that exists beyond all texts or categories. Even the most visible monk in India, His Holiness the Dalai Lama, entitled his most recent major book *Beyond Religion*, to remind us that day-to-day compassion and understanding and attention are not restricted to any one group. As she makes her thoughtful way among these beings of purpose and determination, joining them on their walk, Briana reminds us of what is true beneath all our words and ideas.

Nara, Japan
August 2017

PREFACE

Briana Blasko

The creation of this book has been a truly humbling experience. It has involved a lot of letting go – of expectations from others and myself – and acceptance of others and myself. The people I've captured in the images displayed no particular desire for recognition or fame. This has been enlightening – for what I was *doing* didn't matter to them; rather, they *responded to my focus on being*.

Often, it seems that we have too many things, collections, photographs, documentation. Is all this really necessary, I ask myself again and again. In fact, at various points along my journey, I felt that I was taking too few pictures, and that I might not even be able to make a book. At times, I saw my work more like a sand mandala that I could wipe away, without leaving any trace of the effort or the vision underlying it. For me, there was something intensely beautiful about that. But here I am, writing the preface to this book, hoping to share my journey through this collection of photographs.

It would be helpful to begin at the practical edges, like where I went and who I met and the stories I heard and the impressions they made on me. Over four years, I travelled extensively across India and Nepal and observed the everyday lives of practising Jains, Buddhists, Sufis and Hindus, and a Catholic priest. Jains predominate in the book because I spent the most time with them. I met a group of Jain monks and nuns several times over two years and in different locations, and had the opportunity to join them on their pilgrimages through Kolkata, Jharkhand, Uttar Pradesh, Bihar and, finally, in Indore.

Although I am looking at people who belong to specific religions and carry out traditional practices, this book is not intended to be about religion; rather, it aims to reflect an innate interconnectedness of spiritual lives.

Photographing *silence* and *stillness* in people requires a quieting of the mind on the part of the photographer, as well as an exchange of energy where you can receive the silence; yielding at times a kind of exquisiteness in its simple repetition.

As I followed practitioners of different spiritual traditions, I noticed the calming rhythm of the repetition of movements, stances, prostrations, postures – the hands, feet and extensions of the body moving – a Jain monk waving a white cloth with his arm raised as a symbol of non-violence, or a Buddhist *tokden* blessing someone with his arms outstretched. In the physical reach of the arm, or the bending of the torso with an extension of conscious breath, I observed how the fruition of disciplined *practice* connects with perfection, prayer and blessing.

My earlier book, *Dance of the Weave*, focused on how parts of the body move and form shapes and how external layers of fabric say something about the person inhabiting them. Most of the people photographed in that book were performers who welcomed the chance to be photographed. In this book, there is no performance or performing. It tries to capture the 'real' and 'simple', completely at variance with a performance. There were some individuals I met and photographed who I felt were performing for me; however, I have not been inclined to include those images.

More than anything I feel this work is a personal journey. A journey that perhaps began as an inquiry into my mother's life choices. My mother has chosen a life filled with silence and contemplation, pursuing Buddhist studies on her own. My parents separated when I was five and I grew up with my father. As a child, my mother's world was largely foreign to me. Although I loved spending time in her Buddhist community, it was very removed from life with my father who had brought me up in ways that would allow me to face the world. I kept my mother's life distanced for a long time because her path was so unusual and as a child I didn't see how I could comingle these worlds.

My mother spent several years of my childhood hand-binding books about the Buddhist dharma that were sent to monks living in India. Although she lived in a community, she eventually left it to find her own path. I see my own work here as part of the story of my parents, and many others who are on the path.

All of the people photographed for the book came into my life in an organic way – either as my teachers, or friends of friends who pointed me in a direction. A common thread that ran through all of them was an awareness, energetic lightness of being, compassion and a commitment to their teacher and practices.

In most of the paths depicted in the book, the guru, the teacher, is central to the unfolding of the path, even if the individual eventually decides to leave. Apart from the guru-shishya relationship, there is also the sangha, the community. Sometimes an individual may have his/her own development while the group has a certain perception of the growth that needs to occur. This may hold back the development of the individual. It is not uncommon that as much as a spiritual community can provide support, it can also hold back spiritual growth. For some of the yogis I met, it seemed that they bloomed once out on their own and perhaps returned to a community once they were secure of their growth.

Perhaps because the yogis I met have an understanding of the nature of their minds, I felt a profound connection with them. At ease with themselves, I felt at home in their presence. More and more, I came to understand how people could feel deeply connected to others even when alone – whether through prayer or faith or in the way they express themselves. This is the difference between being alone and feeling a sense of isolation, and experiencing that fundamental sense of solitude and enjoying it.

I did not go to the mountains to seek out yogis, as I did not want to disturb them in their retreat, hence, most of my photographs are of practitioners passing through mainly urban places. There is something comforting in knowing that you can practise your chosen way of being, of finding peace in the inner world, anywhere.

I photographed yogis who were engaged in physical activity and others who were extremely sedentary. These two different aspects – of stillness and movement –appear to be in constant dialogue. Even when silent and still, those who have found inner peace can make a profoundly transformative impact on those around them.

I, an 'outsider', learnt to be fast and tried to capture their essence in as few pictures as possible. Their lives are usually very quiet and they prefer to be left alone. This has changed the way I photograph people.

Over time, taking a picture has become an afterthought. I journeyed to faraway places, and then sometimes decided to not take a picture at all. In photography, if you don't take a picture it's as if the event did not happen, but there seems to be a part of me that believes that sometimes not taking a picture is just as valuable. In some really precious moments, I chose to be with someone and simply experience their presence, without taking a photograph. The compilation of this book also reflects this – of going back and forth between doing something and not doing something. The title *Within Without* in a way represents this do or don't that is constantly happening in every moment. For me this book is a way of sharing my journey of spiritual inquiry; it's value lies in the quiet experiences with people, listening to their stories and feeling their spirit. This is what I hope to give to you.

(The main content from this article is from an interview between Tsering Gellek and Briana Blasko at Ratna Ling, California, in July 2016. Many of the concepts and ideas in the piece came about through the guidance of Tsering Gellek.)

Butterfly

this yellow and black butterfly
uses her dusty wings to push
the air past
the dancing Bodhi leaves

she goes up and up
only to find an empty nest.

Tsering Palmo Gellek

PRACTICE

Following practitioners of different spiritual traditions, I noticed the calming rhythm of the repetition of movements, stances, prostrations and postures. In the physical reach of the arm, or the bending of the torso with an extension of conscious breath, I observed how the fruition of disciplined *practice* connects with perfection, prayer and blessing.

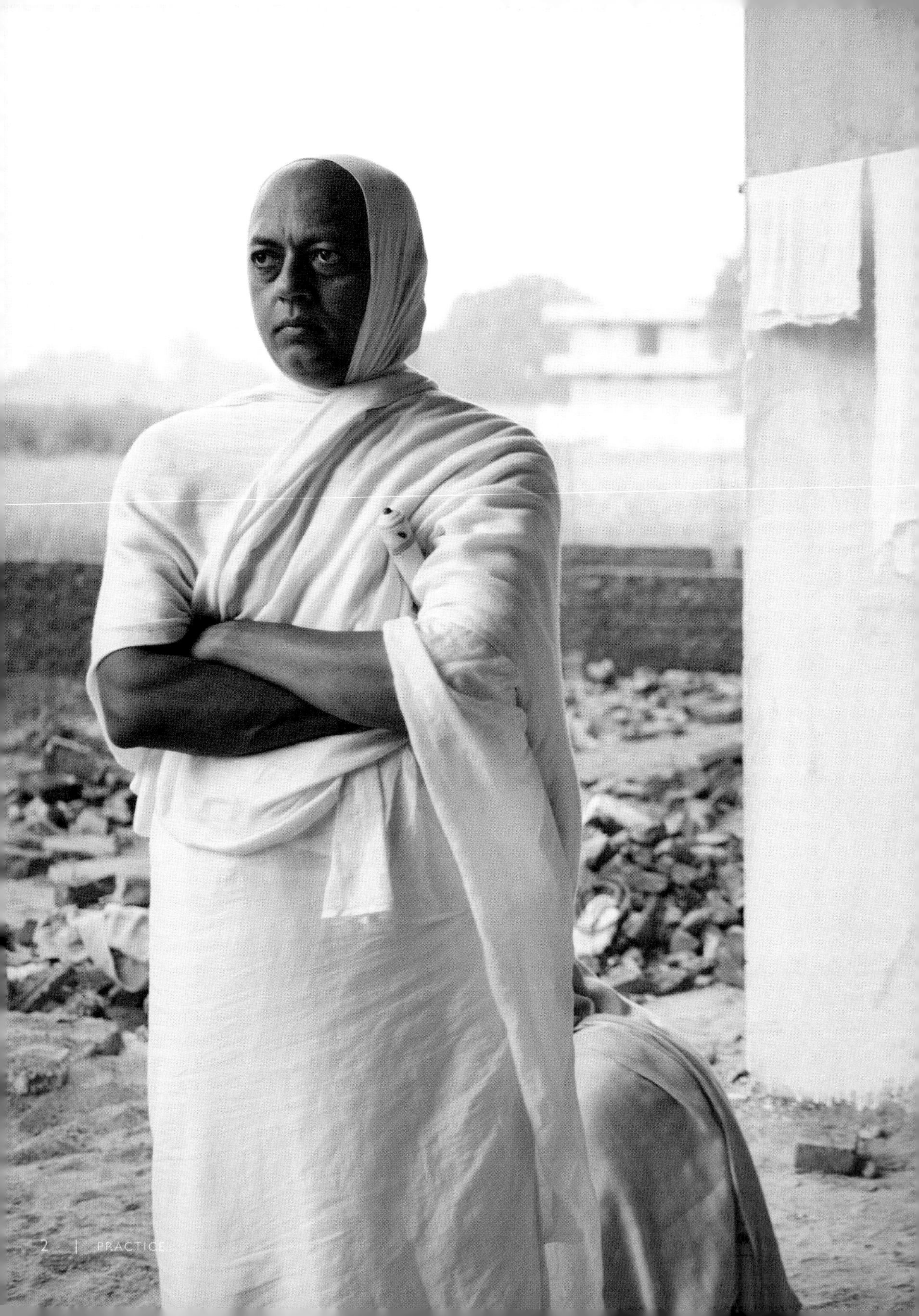

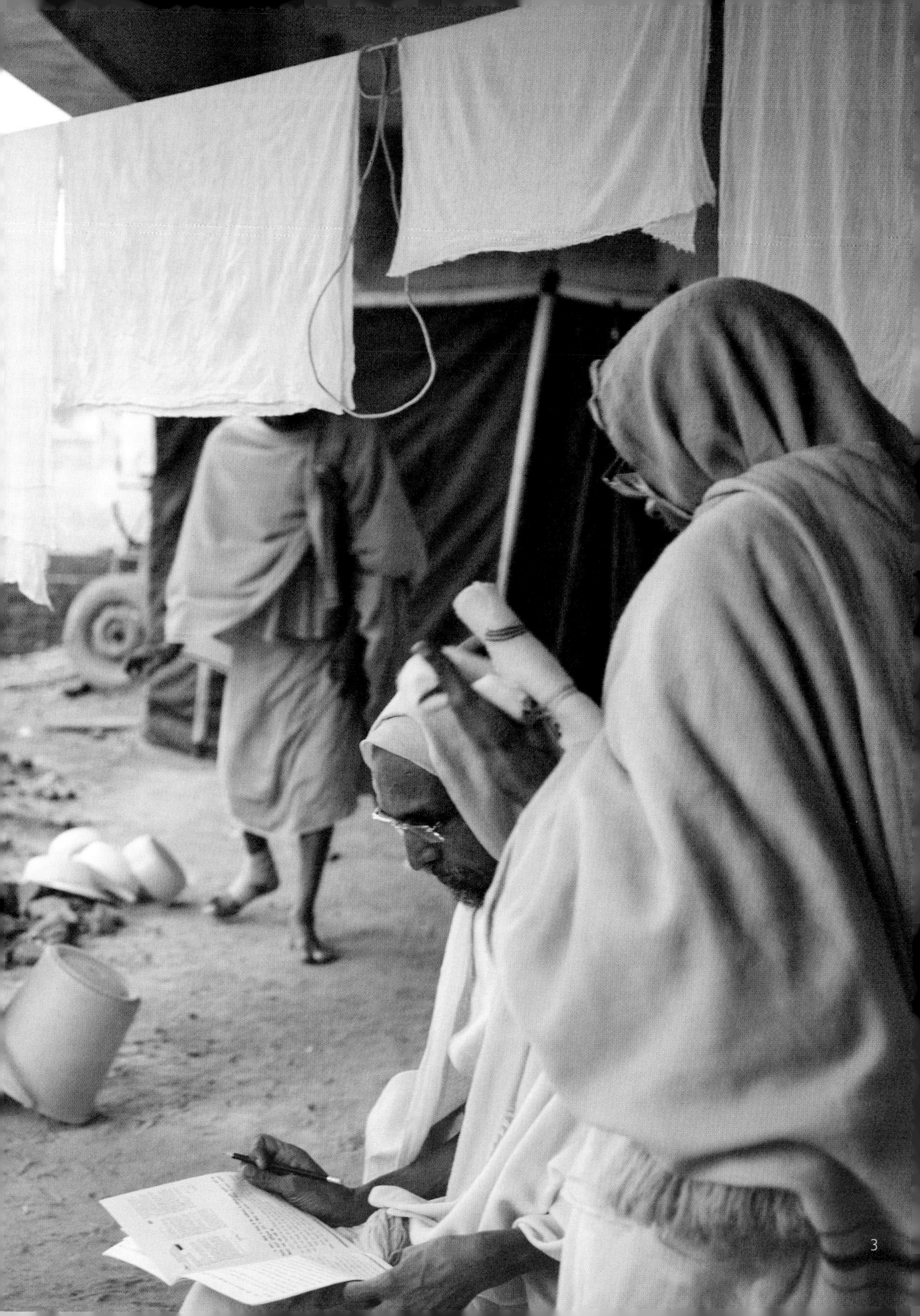

Muni Samvegayash Vijay Maharaj,
Uttar Pradesh, 2016

PAGES 2–3
Swetamber Jains on Vihar,
Uttar Pradesh, 2016

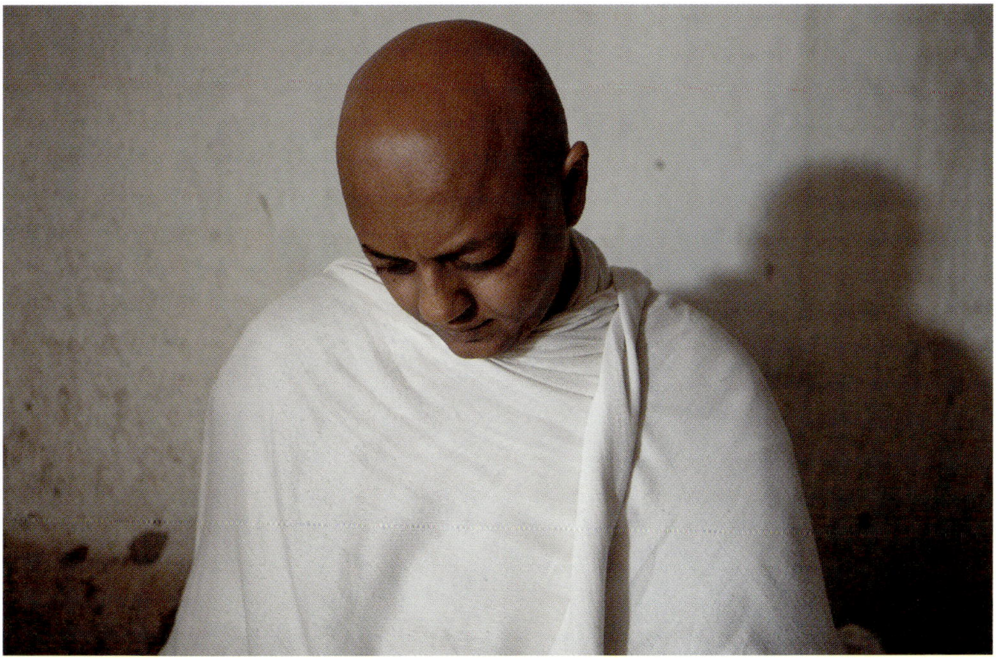

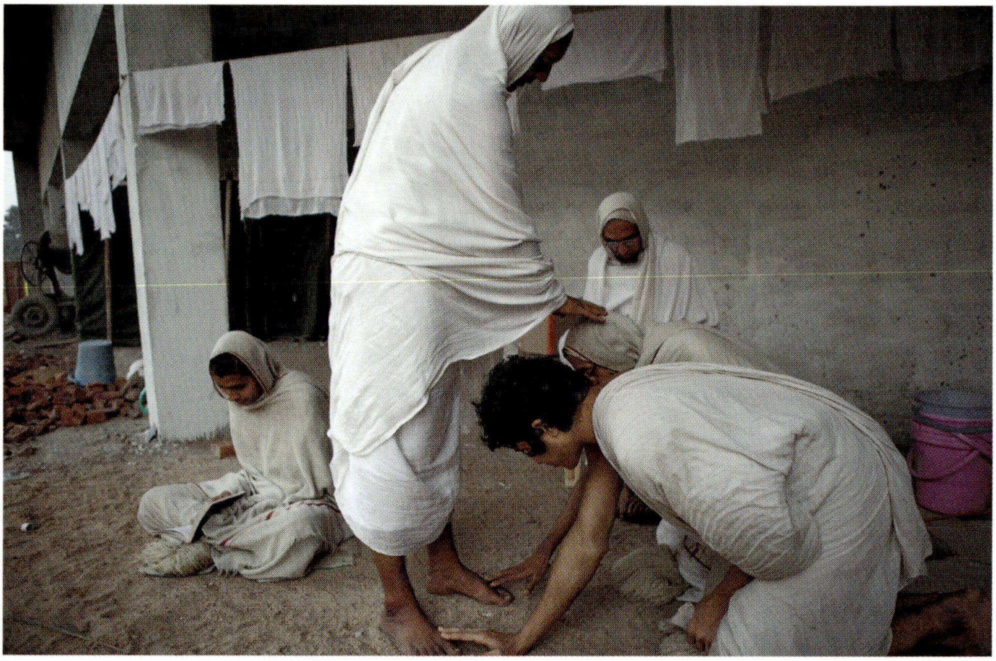

Swetamber Jains on Vihar,
Uttar Pradesh, 2016

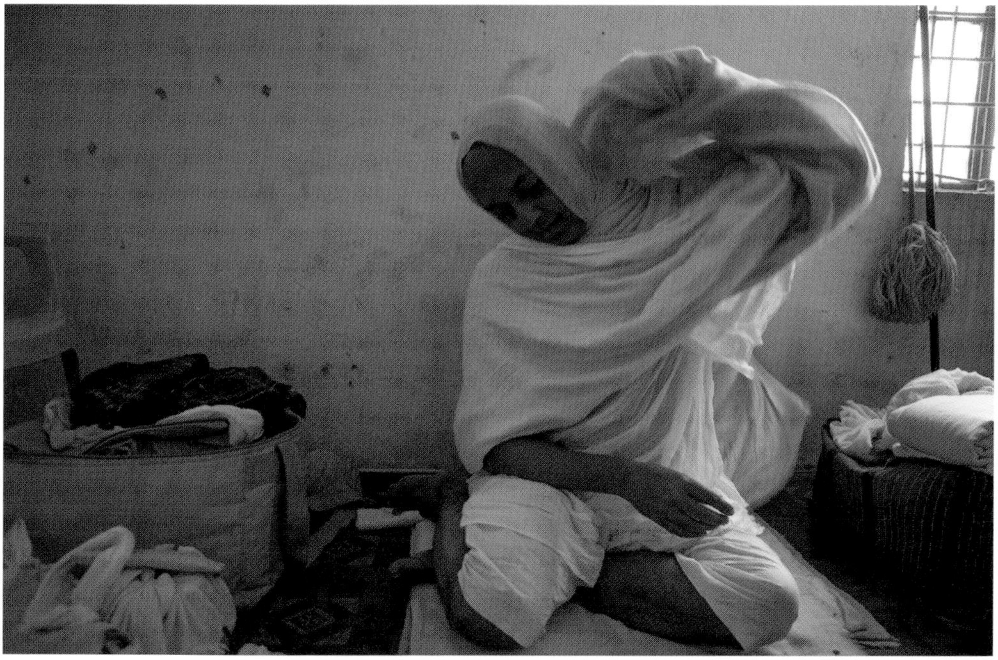

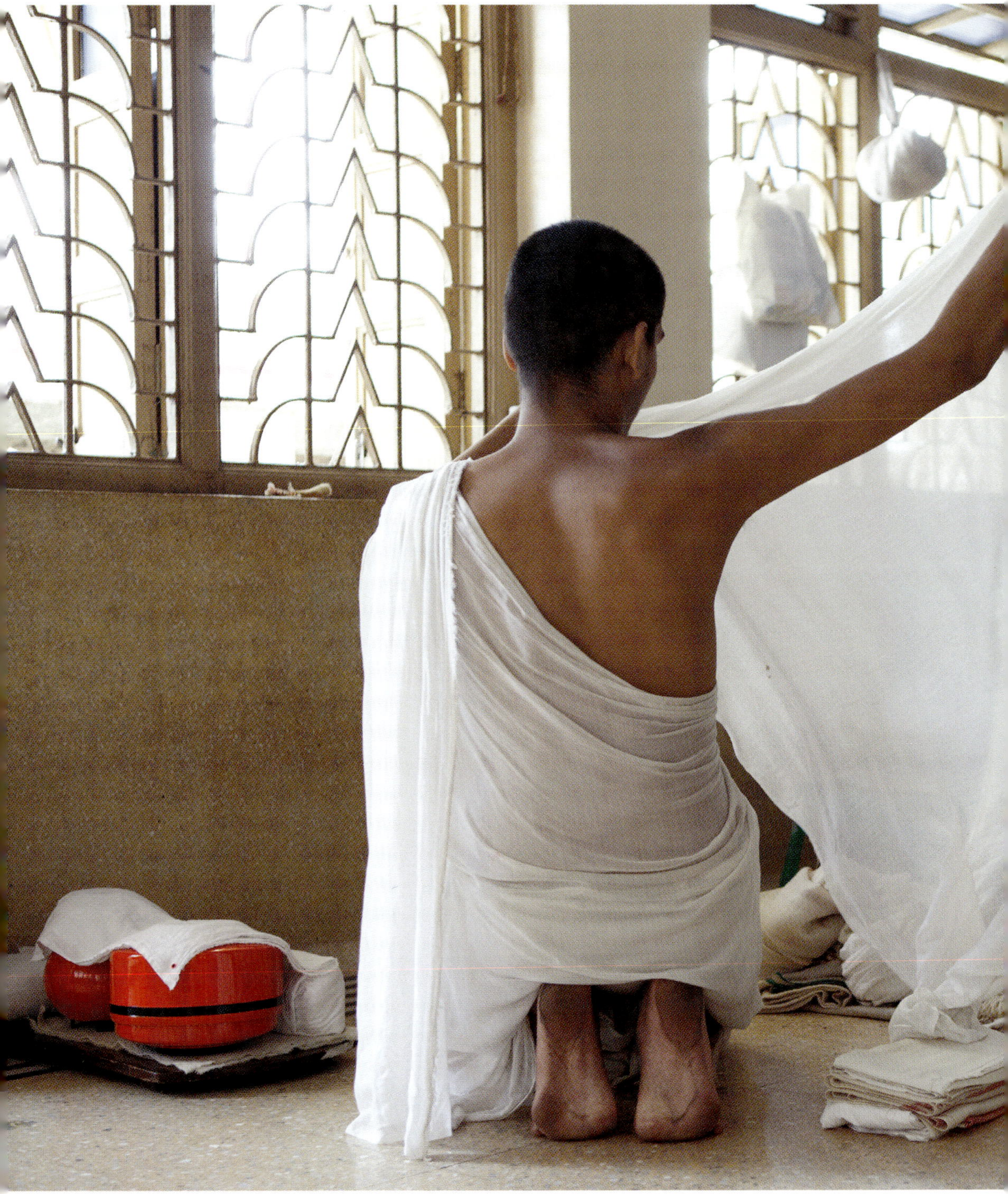

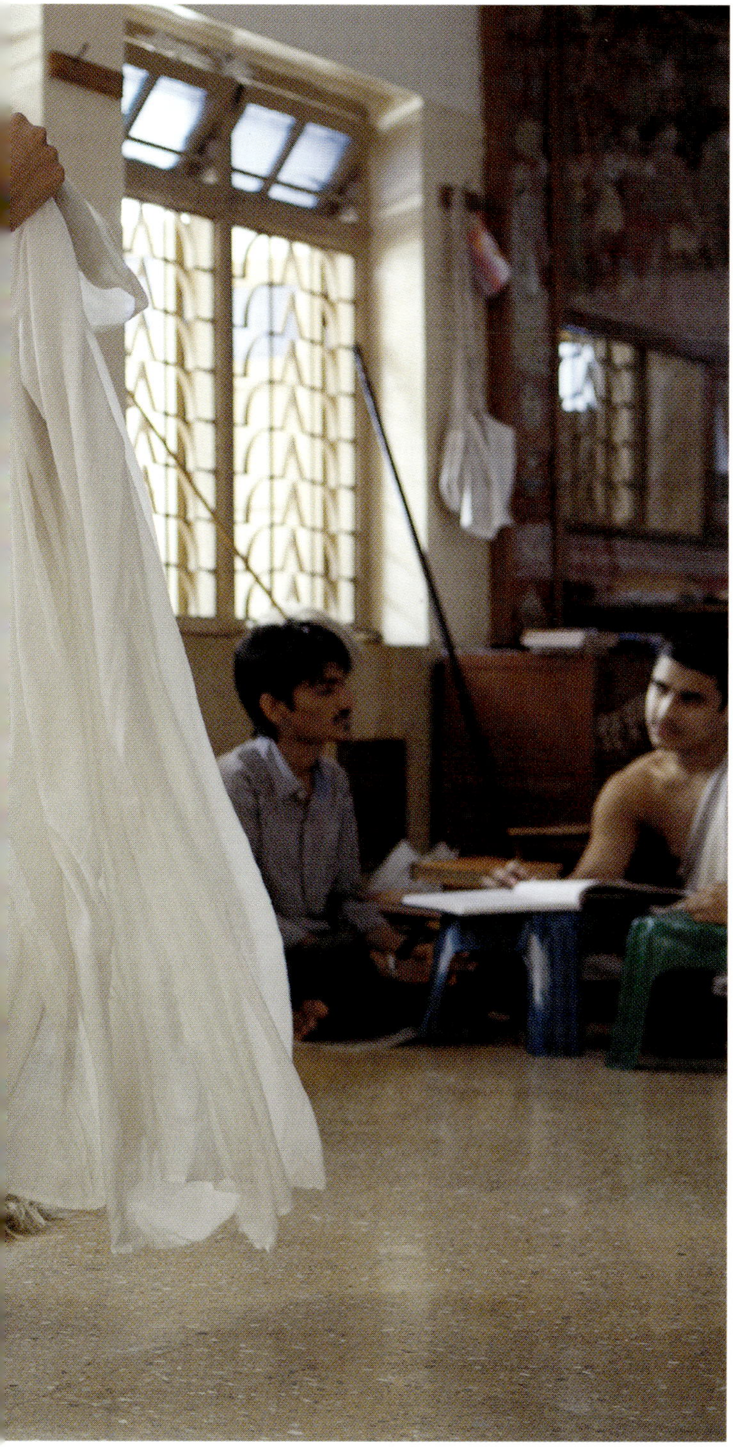

Swetamber Jains,
monsoon season,
Kolkata, 2015

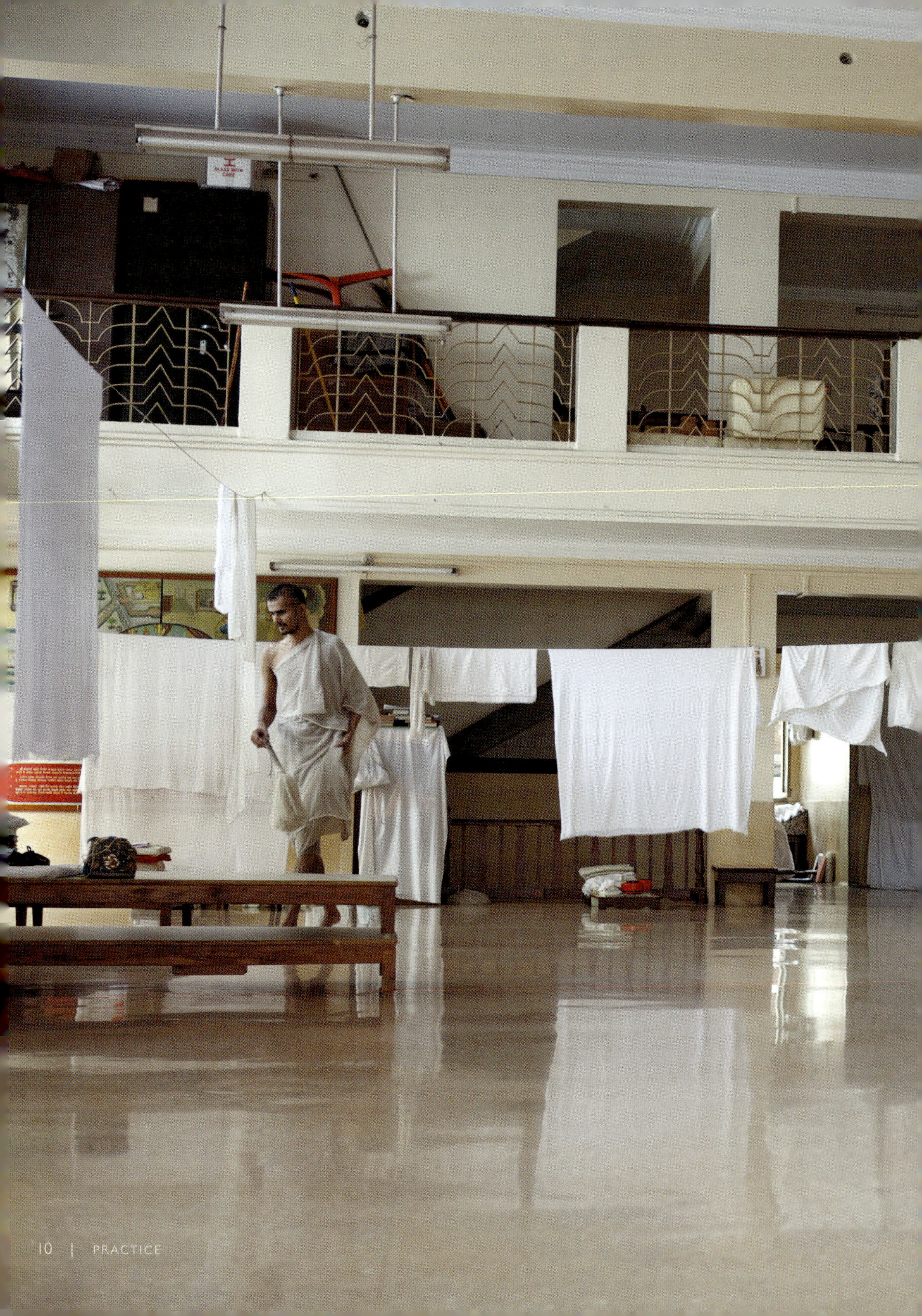

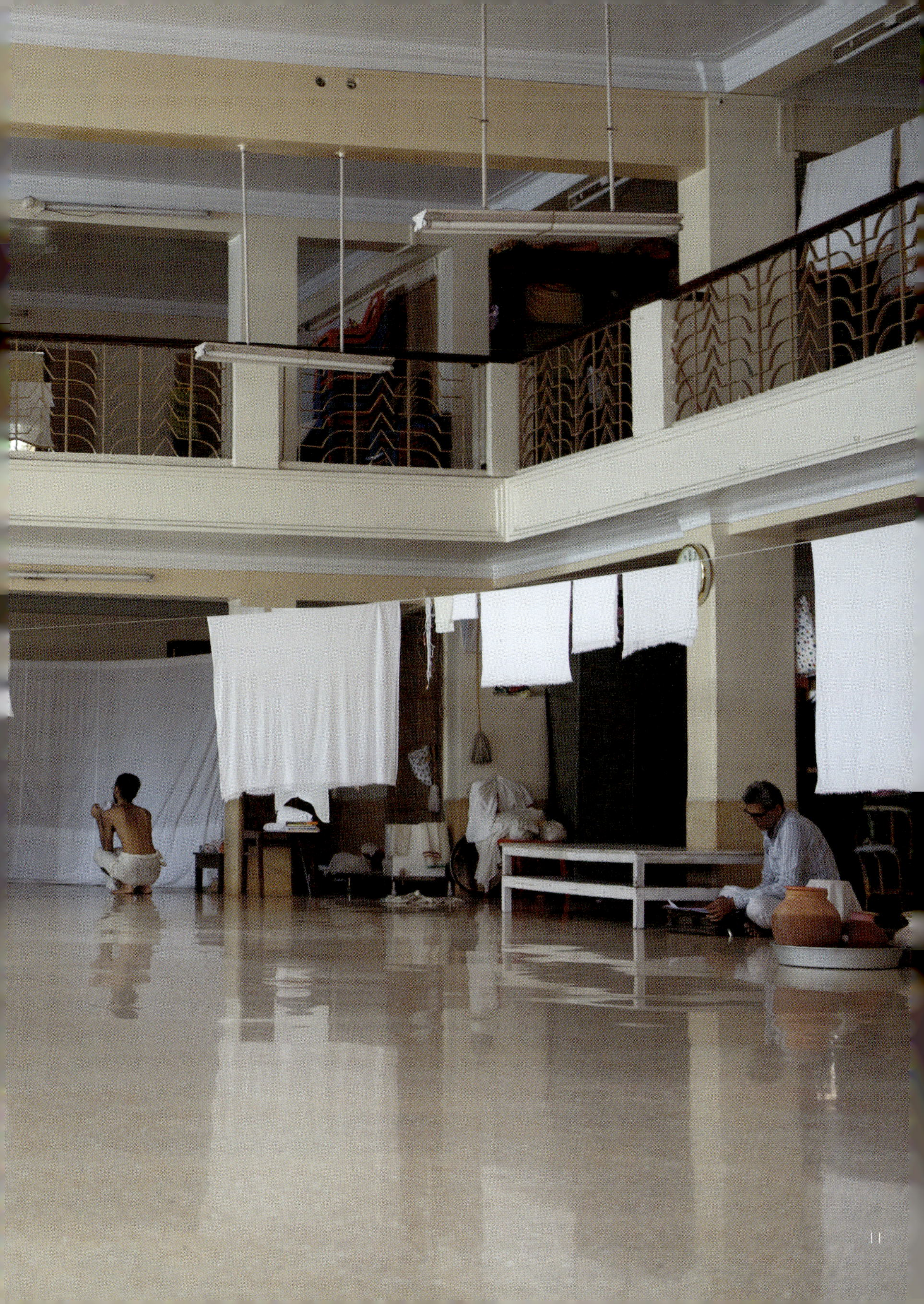

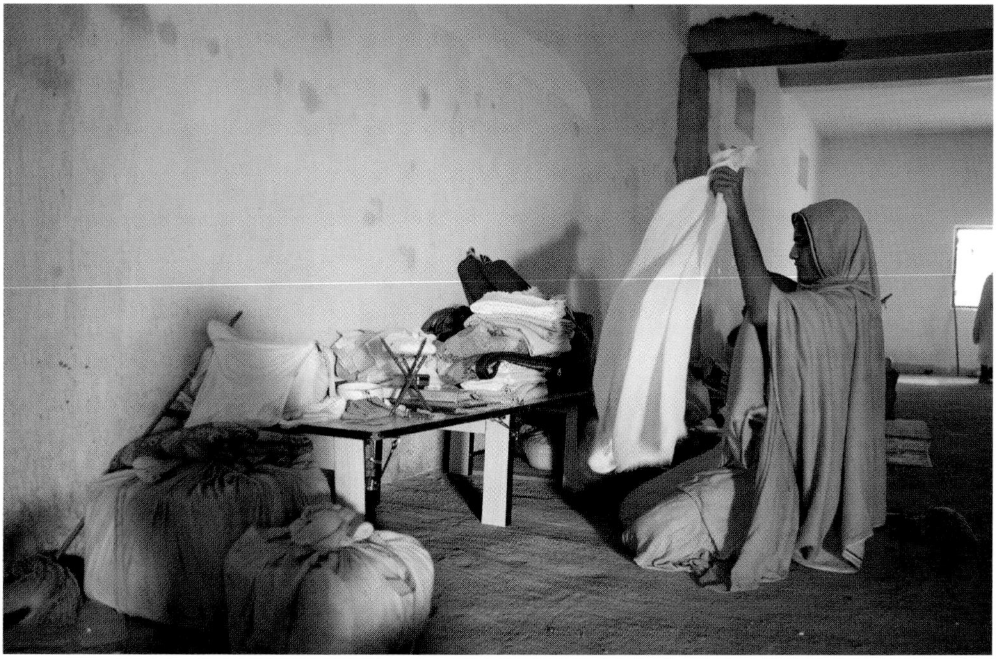

Swetamber Jains on Vihar,
Jharkhand and Bihar, 2016

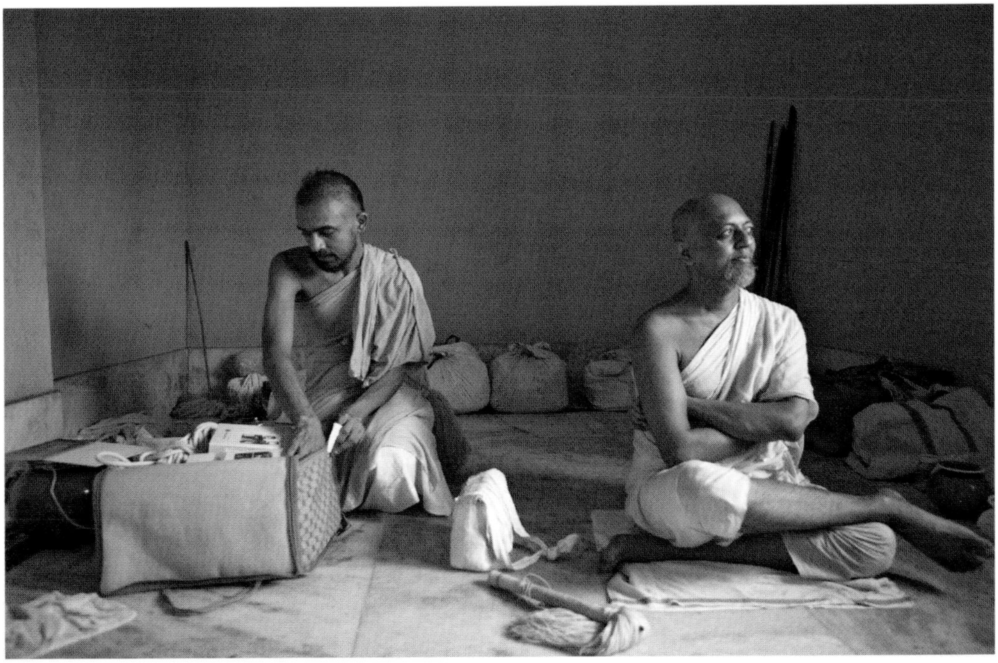

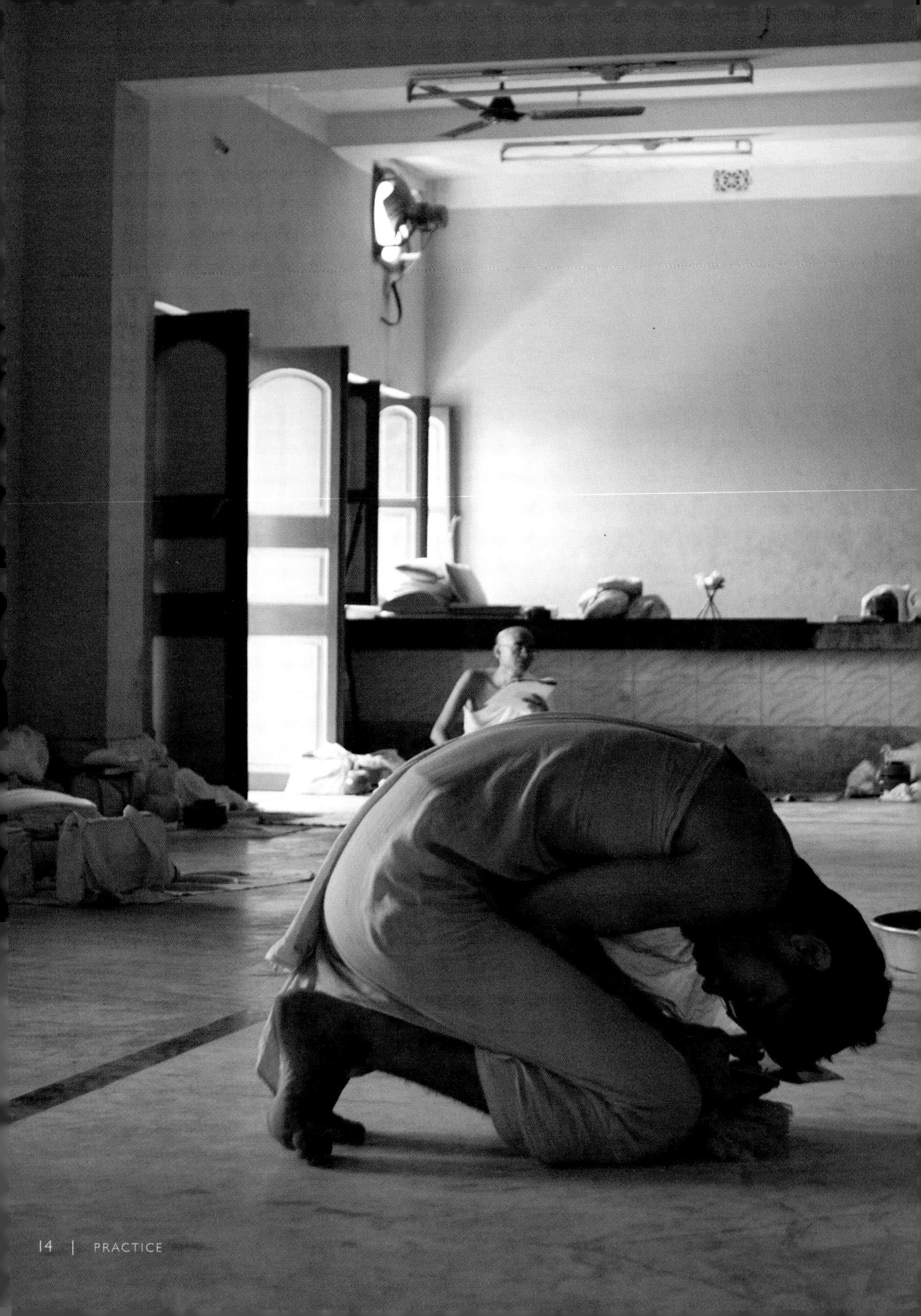

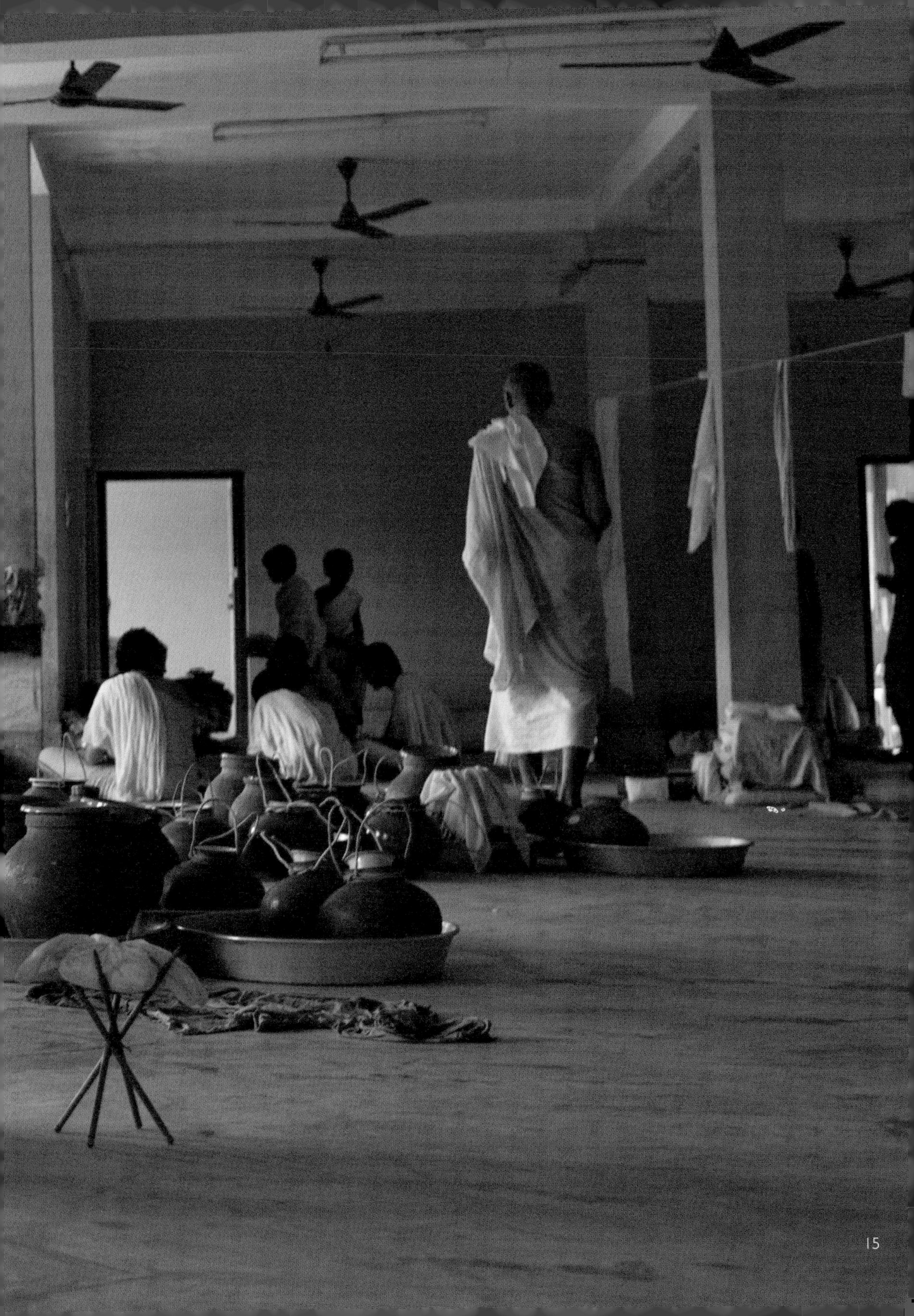

Ashtanga Yoga students,
International Chandramauli Charitable Trust,
Varanasi, 2016

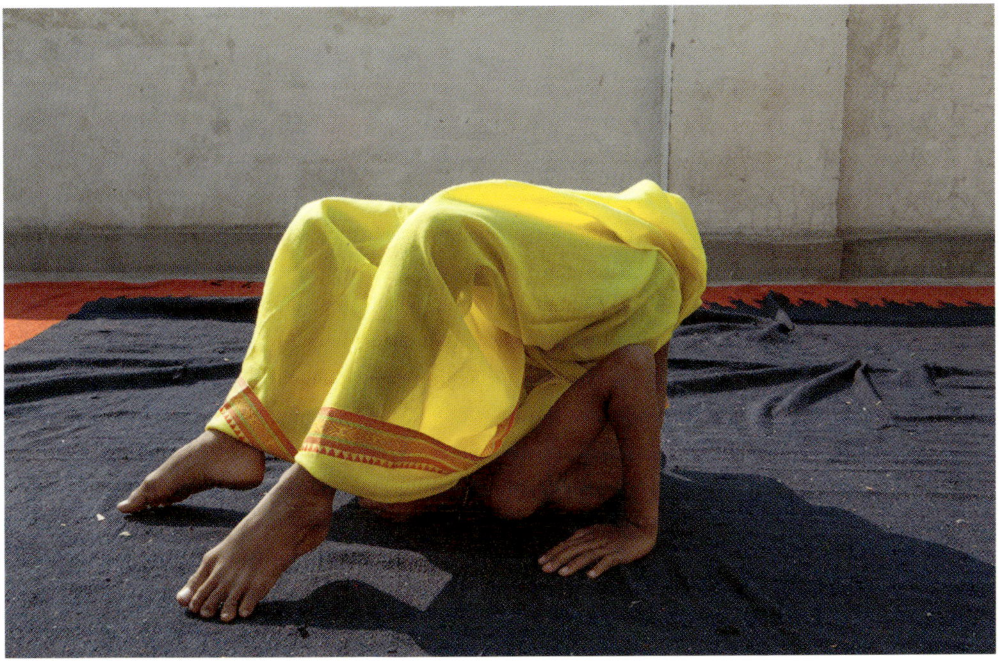

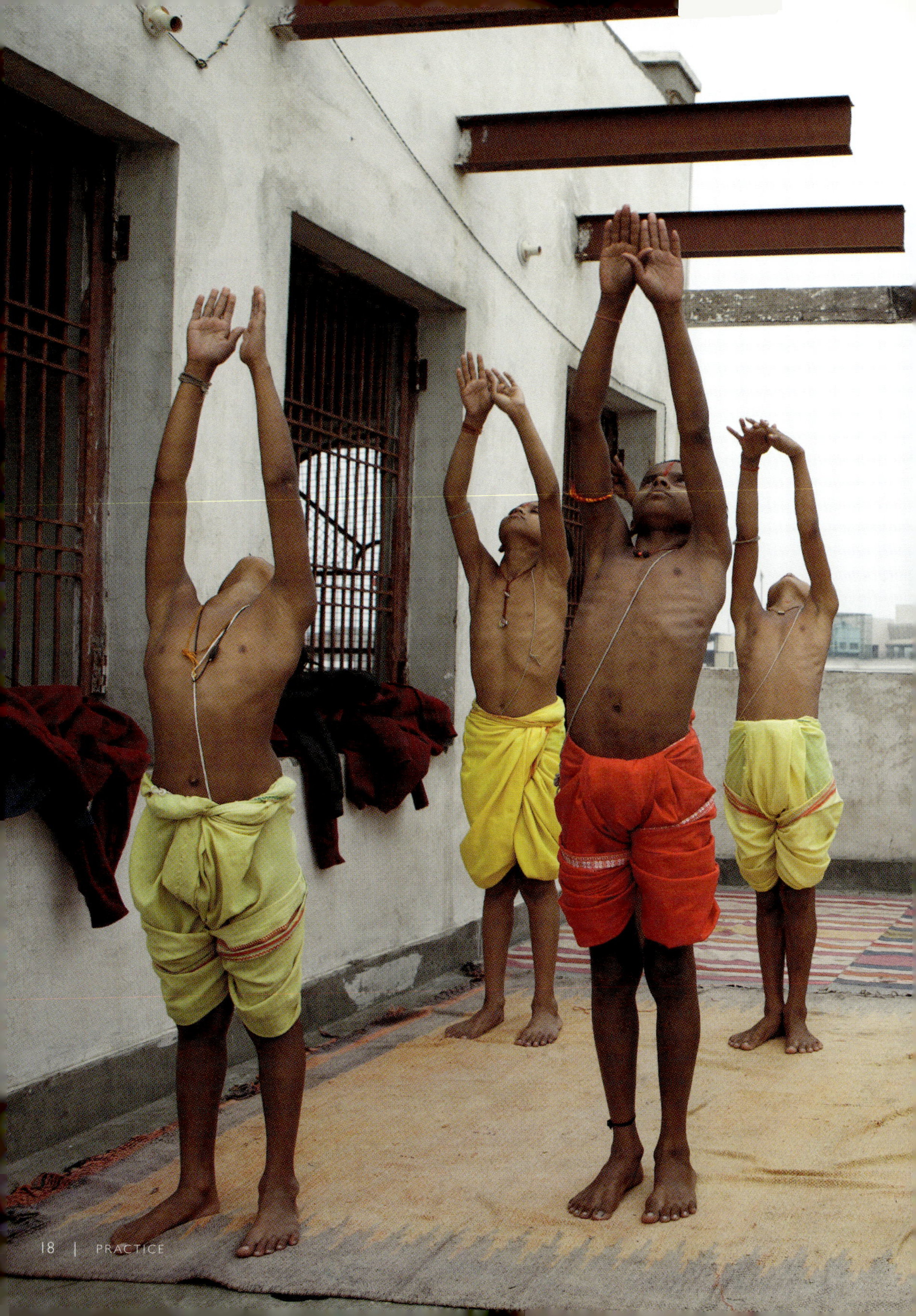

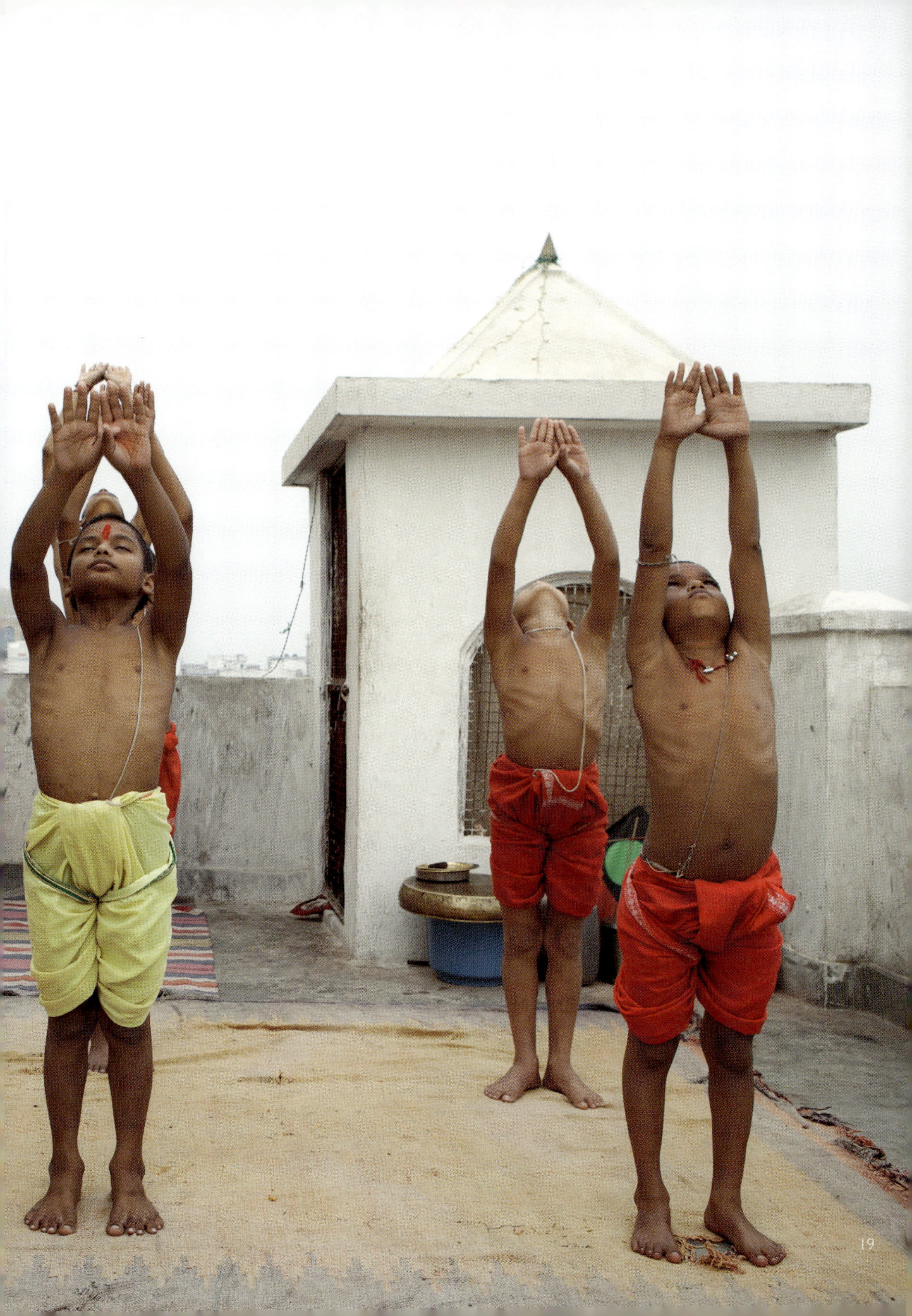

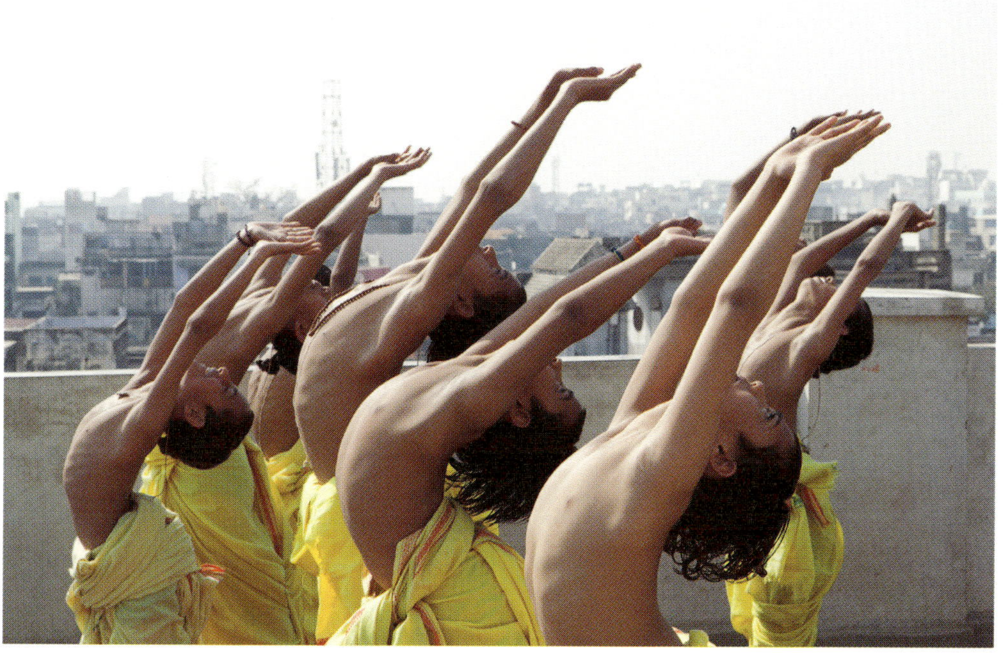

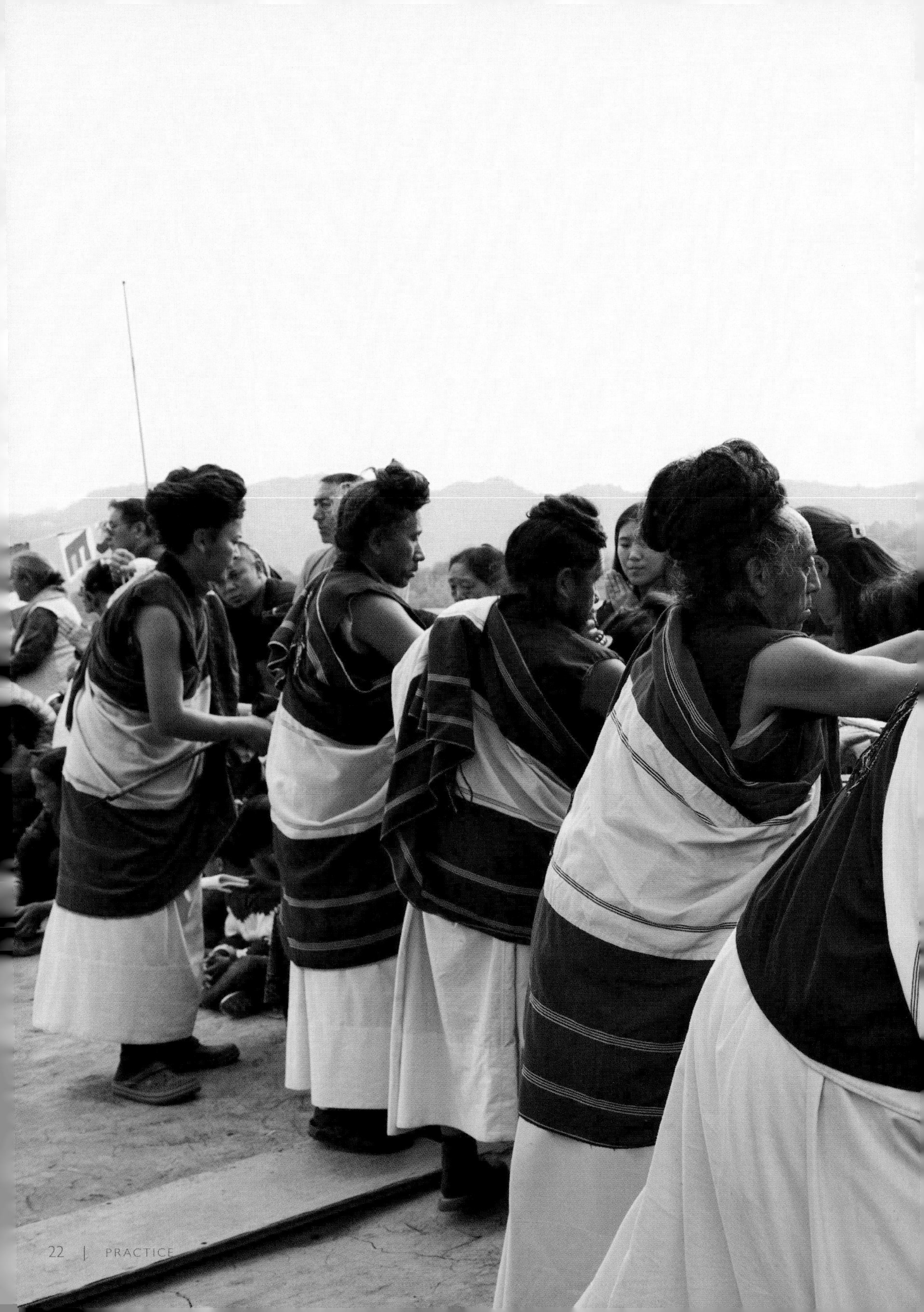

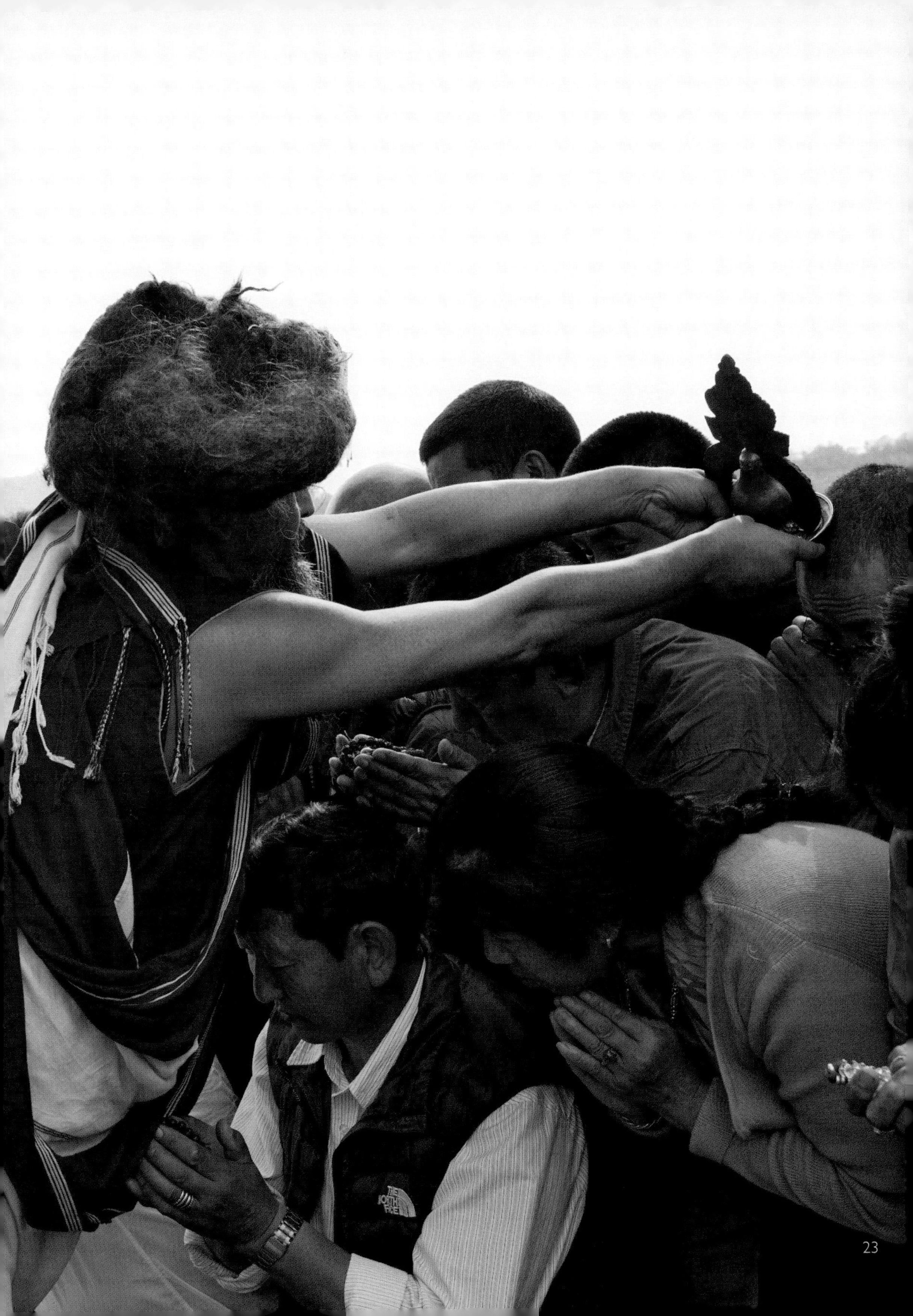

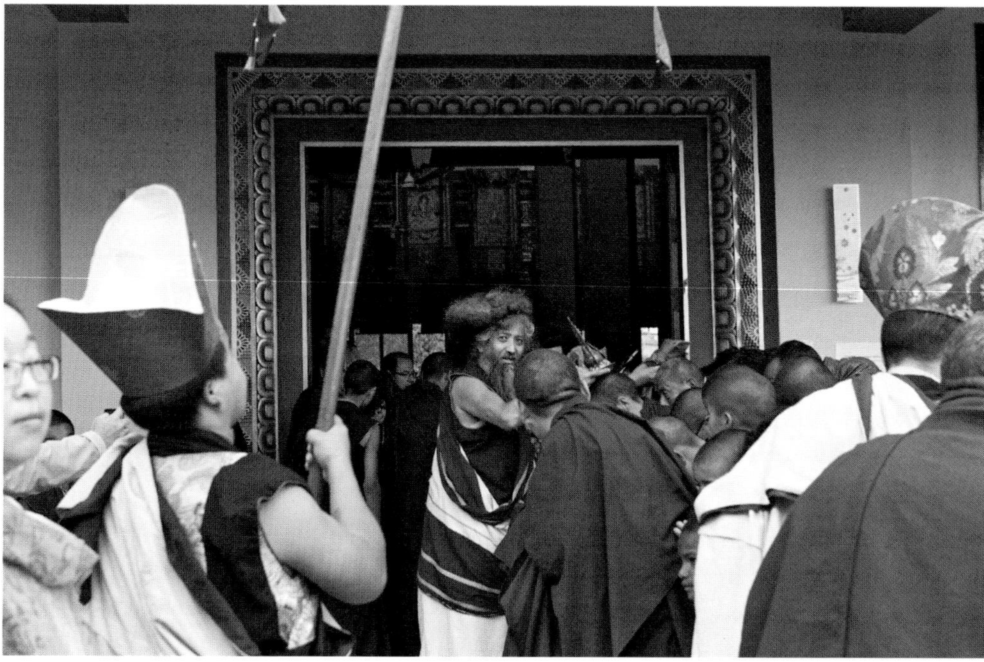

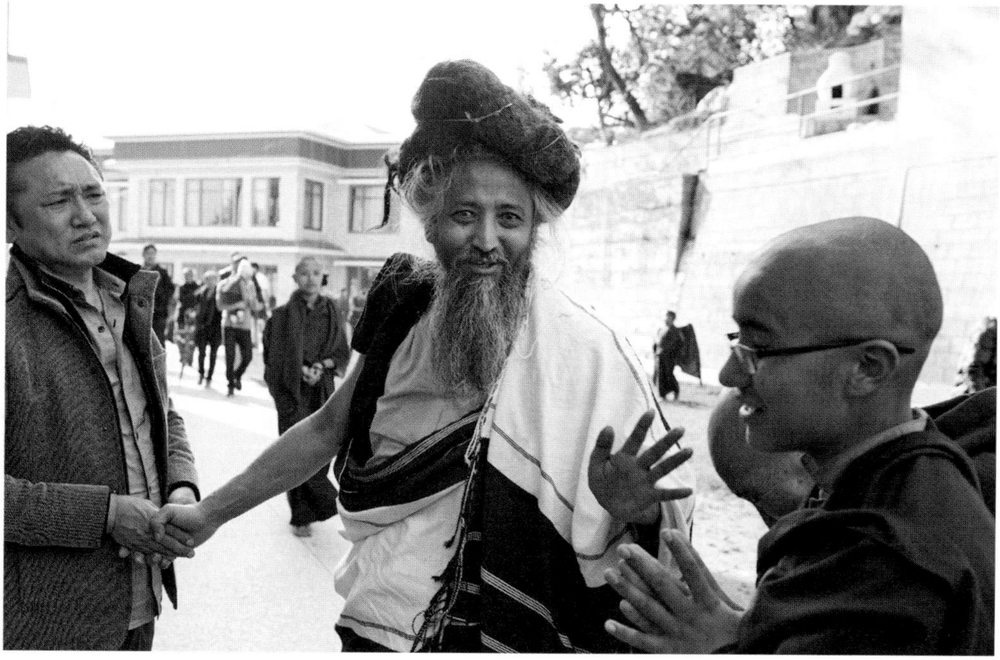

Tokden Thinley Kunchap, after twenty years of strict retreat, came out to offer blessings at the Festival of Lama Dances, Tashi Jong, Palampur, 2016

PAGES 22–23

Tokdens giving blessings during the annual Festival of Lama Dances and Empowerments, Tashi Jong, Palampur, 2016

THE BELOVED

As the practitioner delves deeper into practice, a sense of connection to others grows. The words of the contemplative – frugal, light, often joyful – are treasured exchanges.

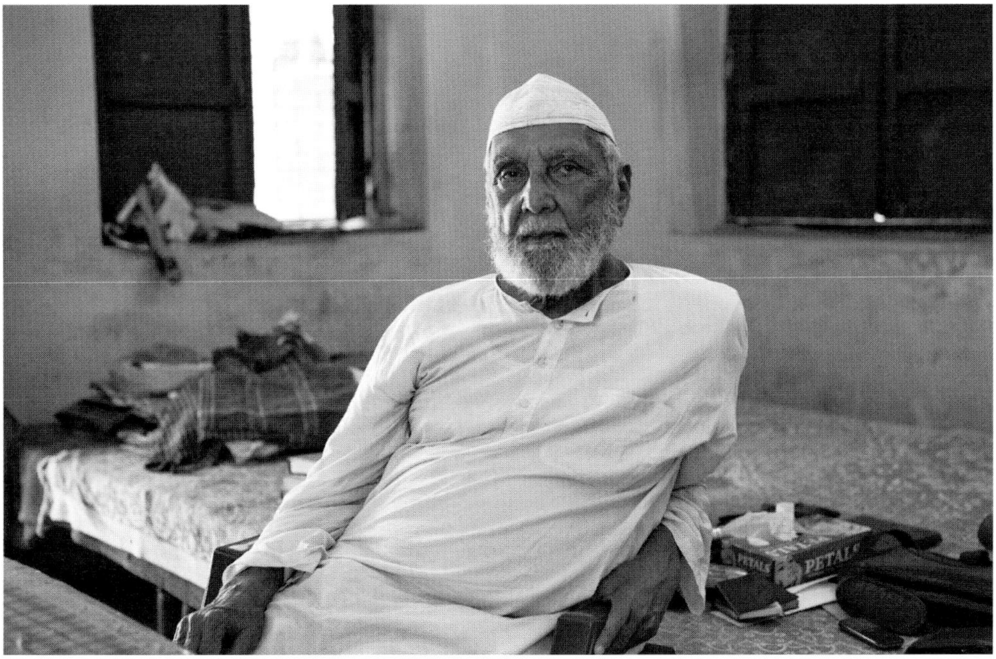

Maulana Jalaluddin Abdul Mateen in his room,
Farangi Mahal Residence, Lucknow, 2016

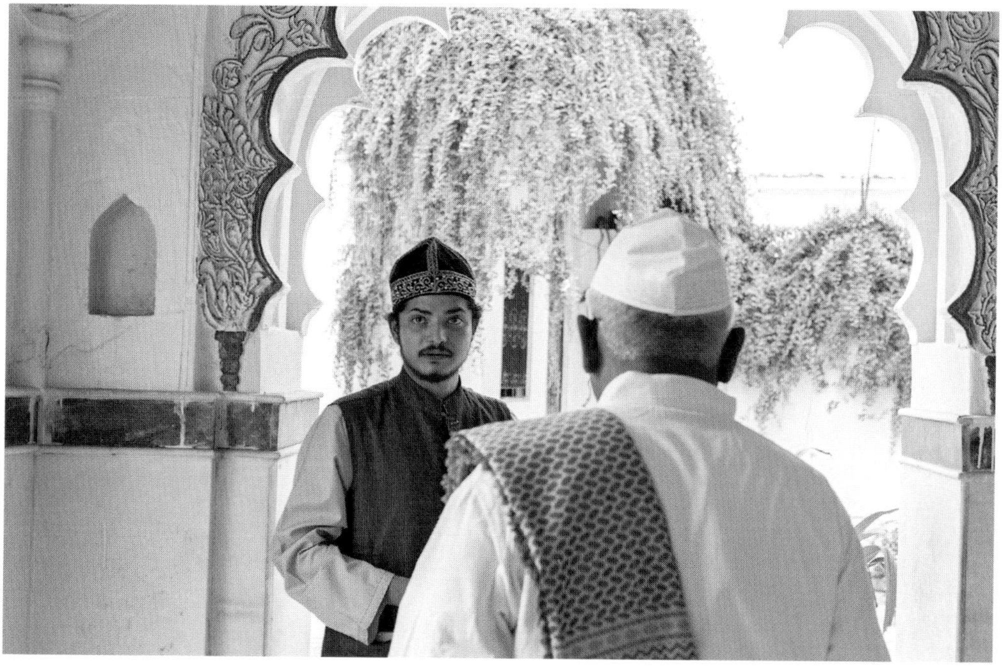

Shah Syed Hasnain Baqai,
Safipur, 2016

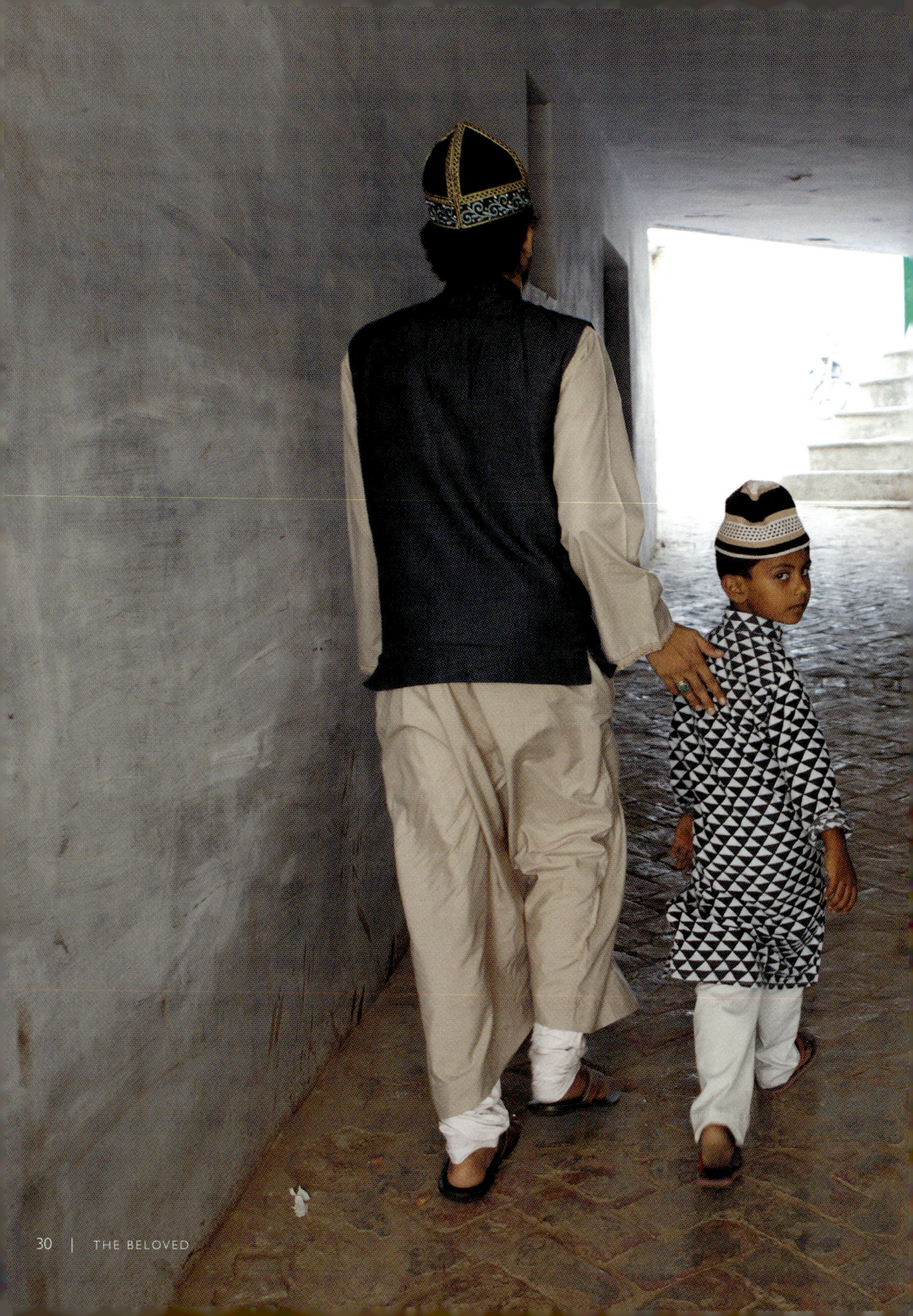

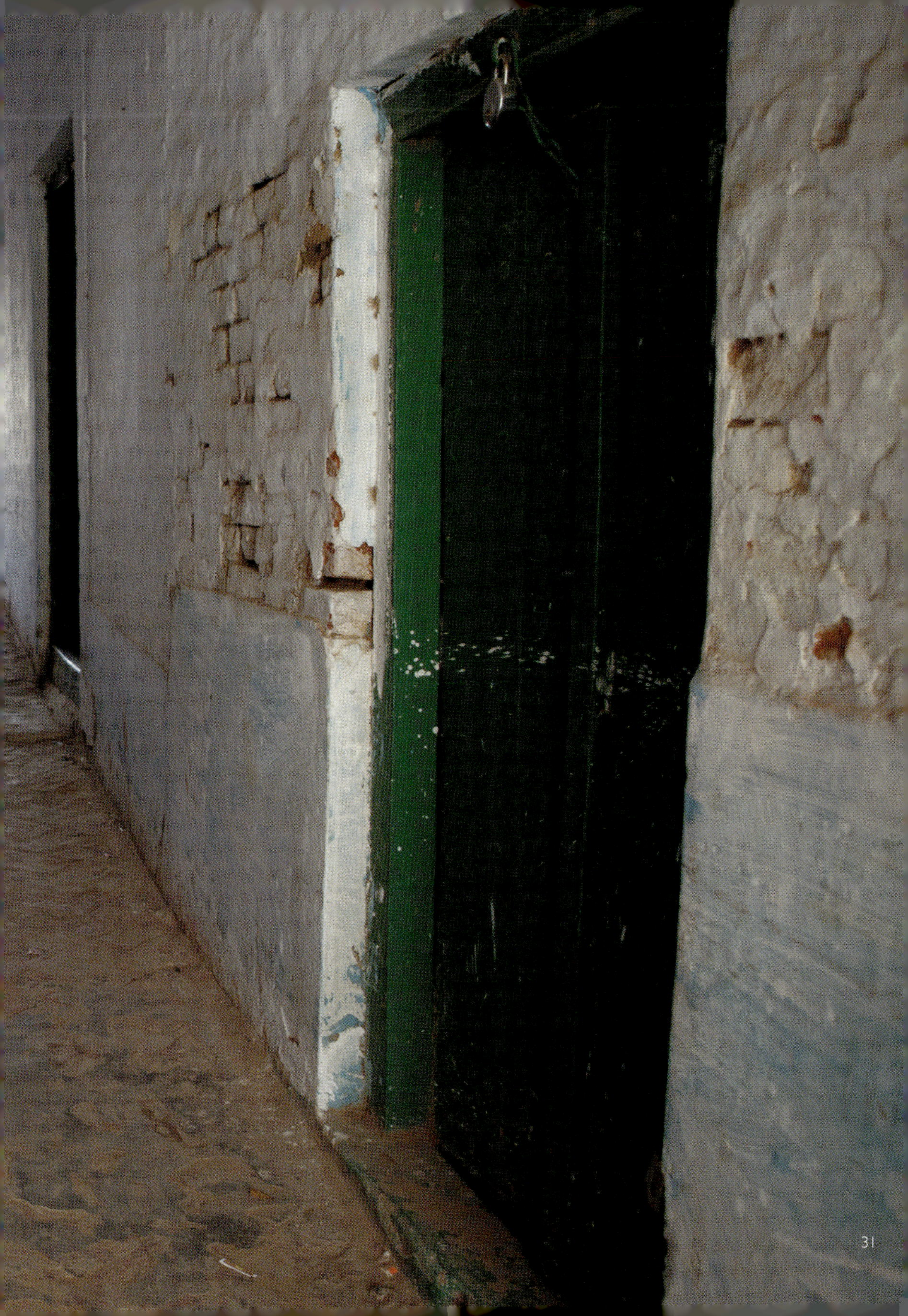

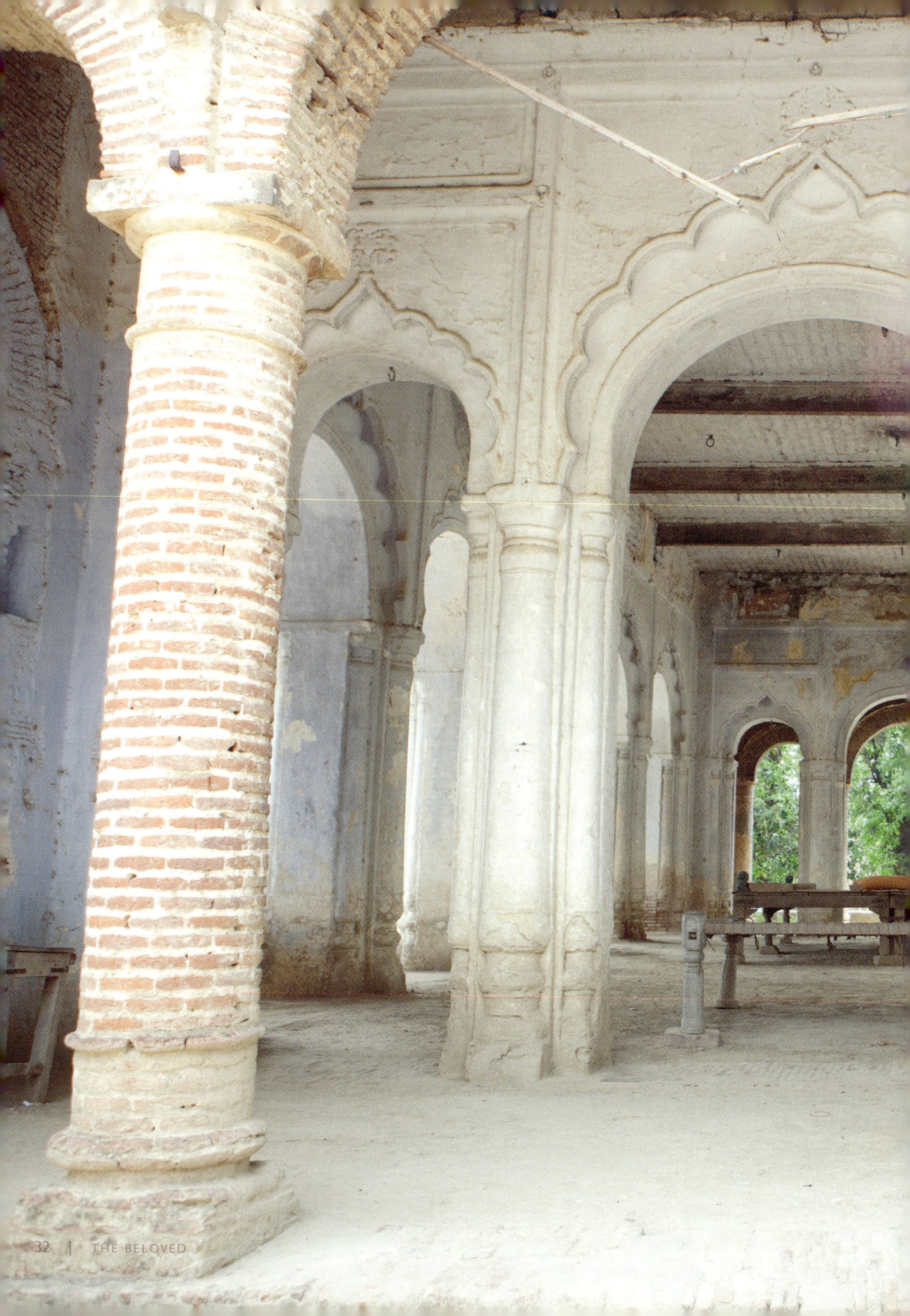

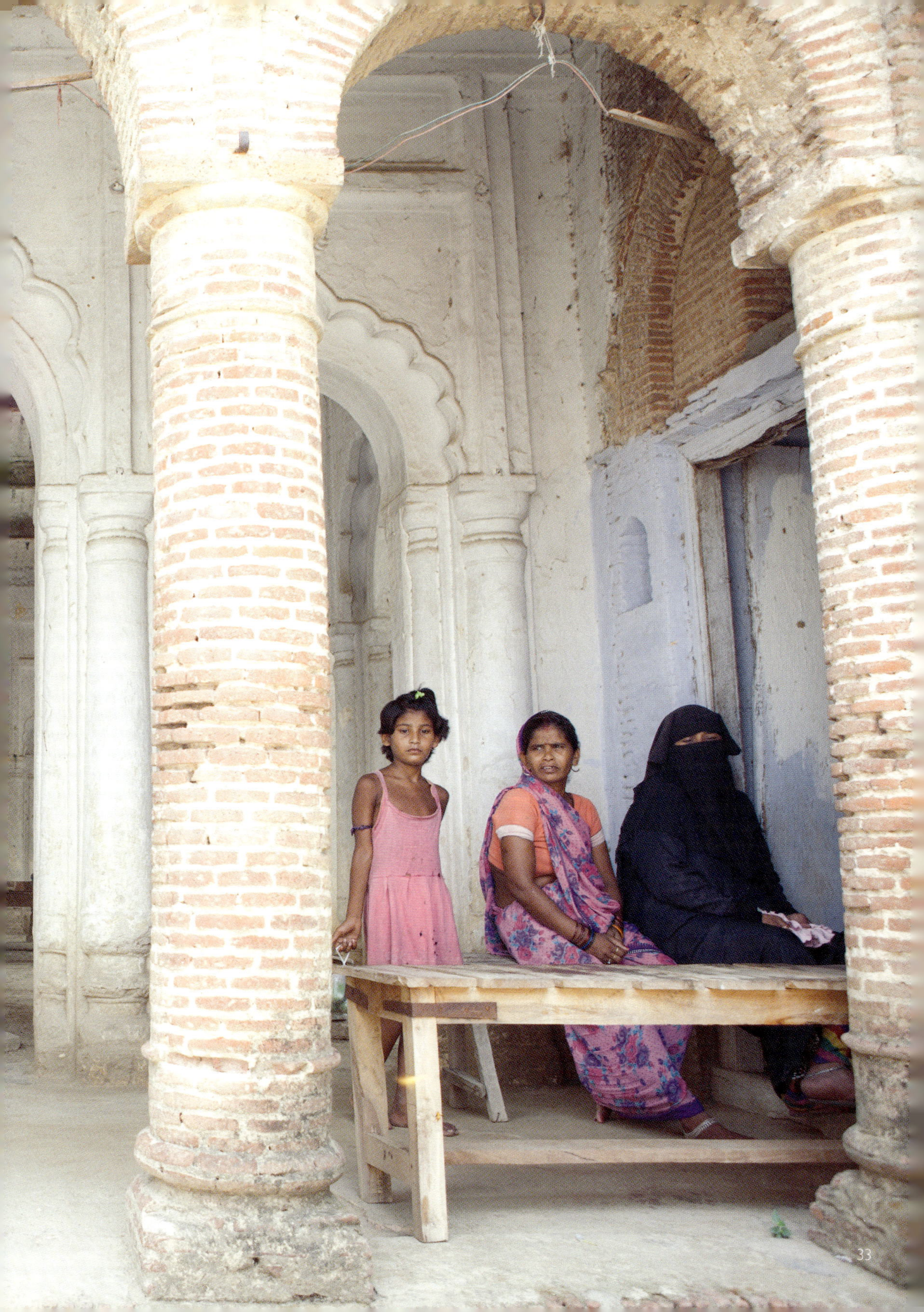

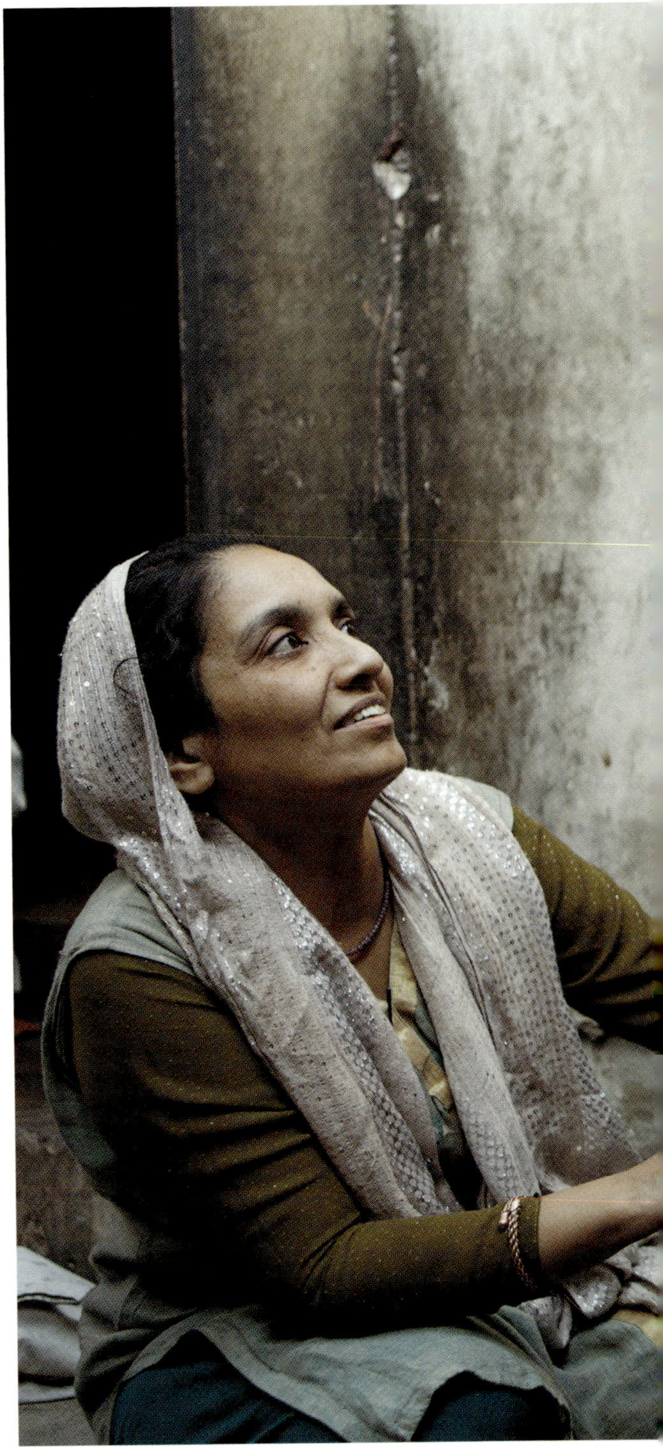

Mohd Jamin Qureshi and
his daughter Reshma,
Jaipur, 2016

PAGES 32–33
Kakori Shrine, 2016

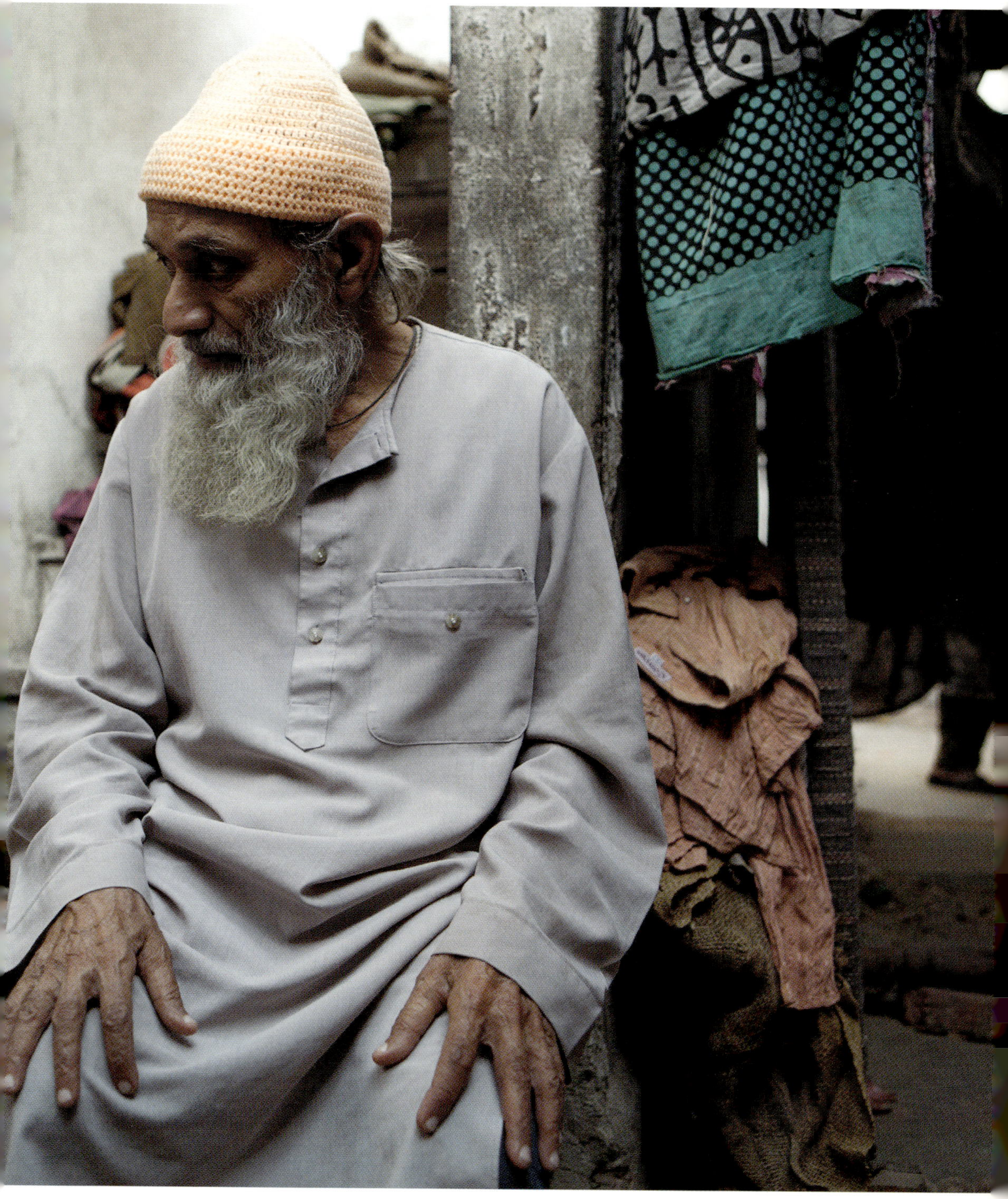

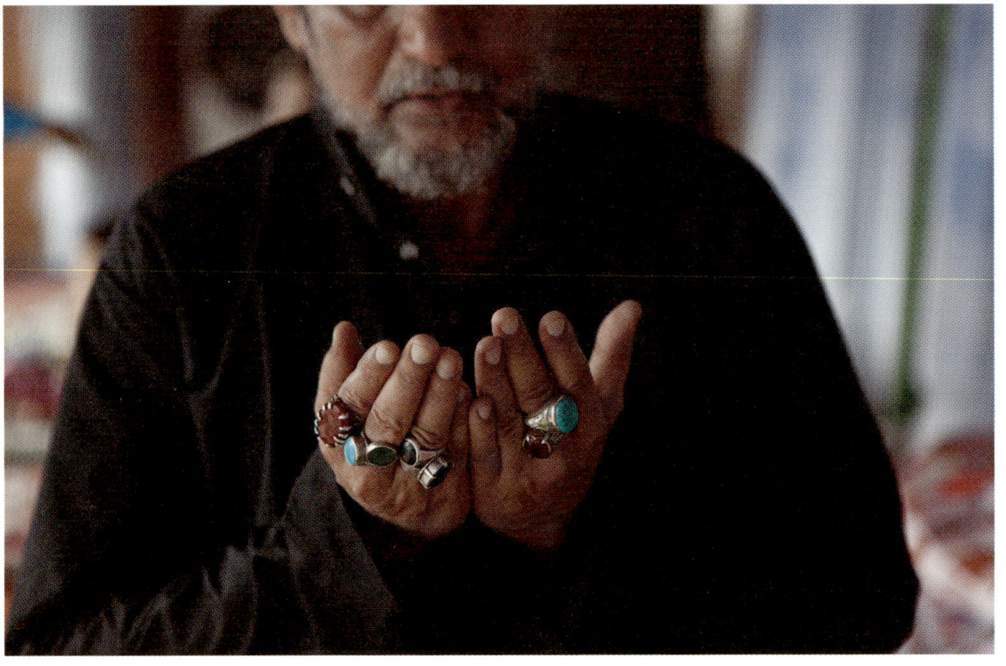

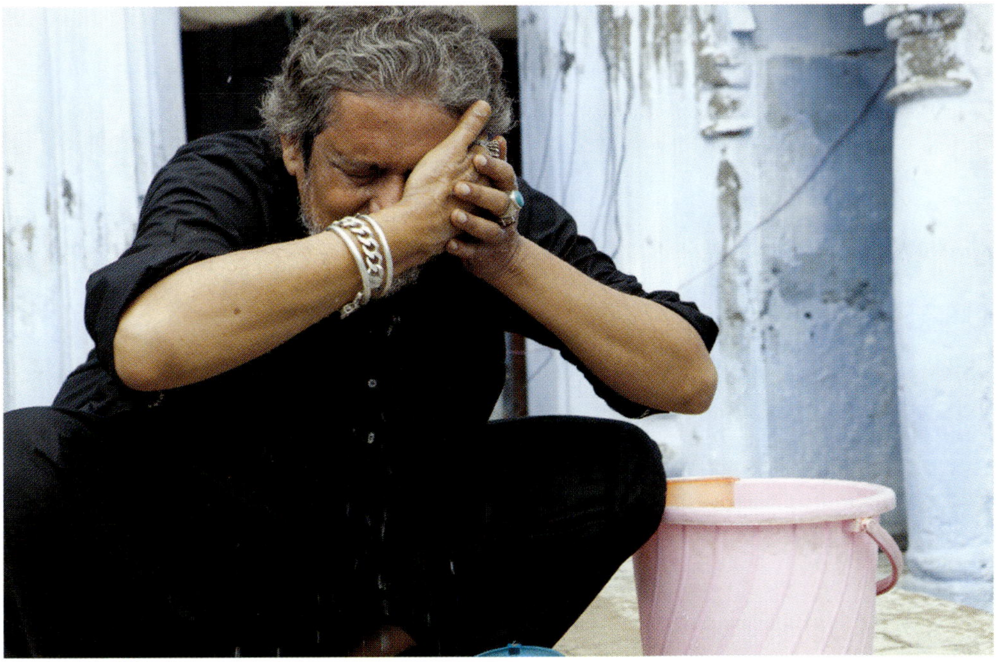

Peerzada Anwar Rahman Jilani,
Sajjada Nasheen of Khanqah Haqqaniya Asiwan,
in prayer at his residence,
District Unnao, 2017

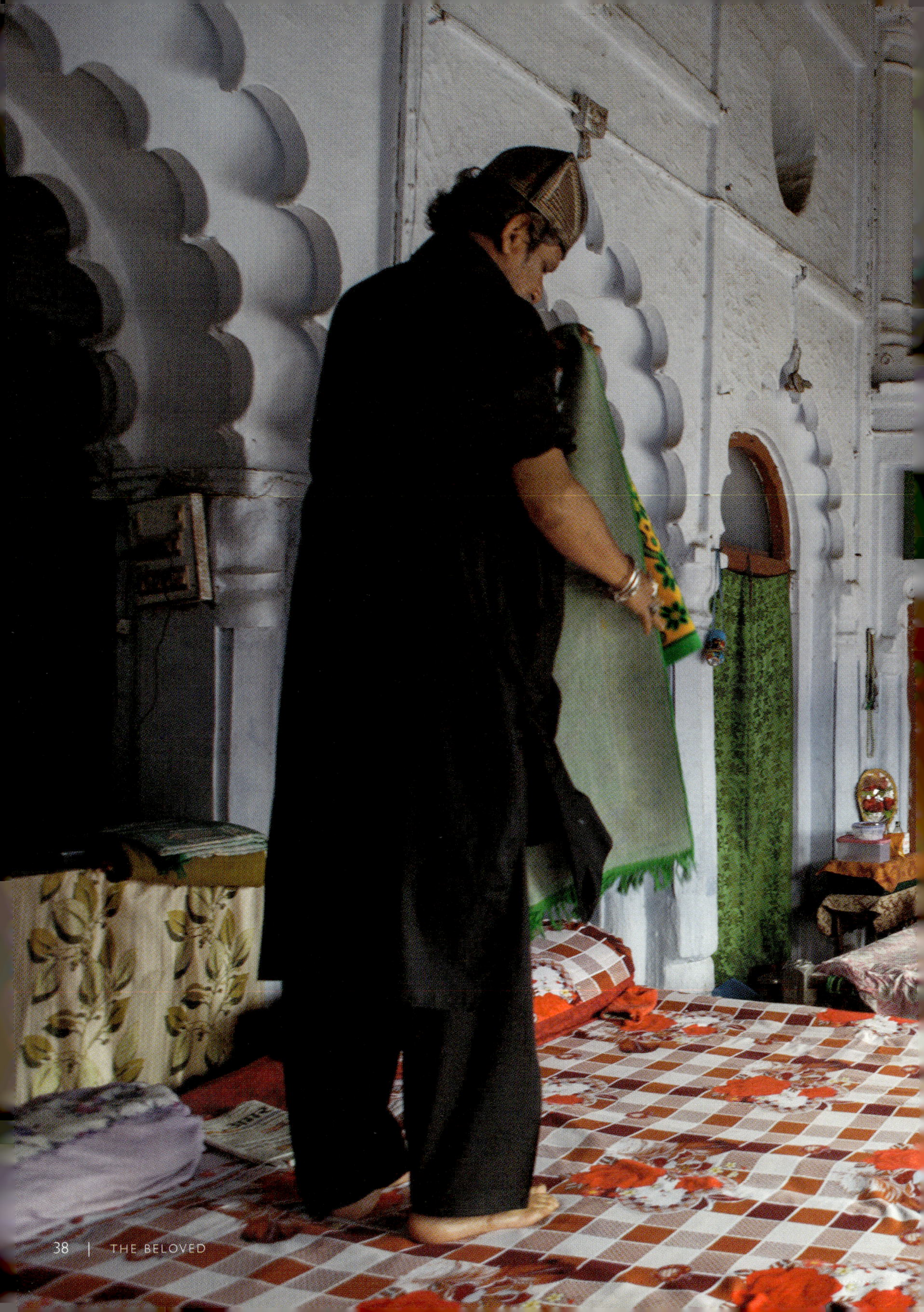

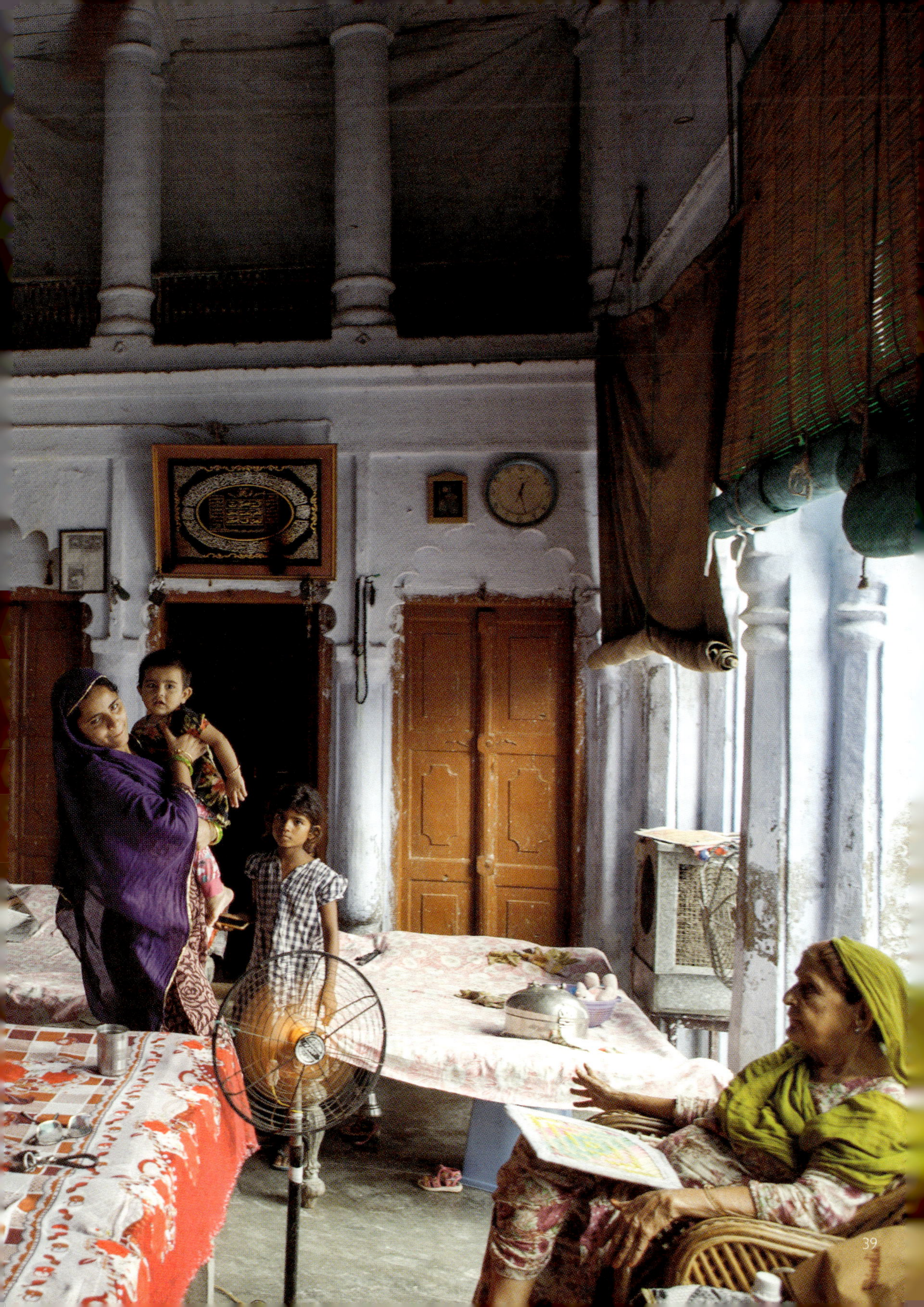

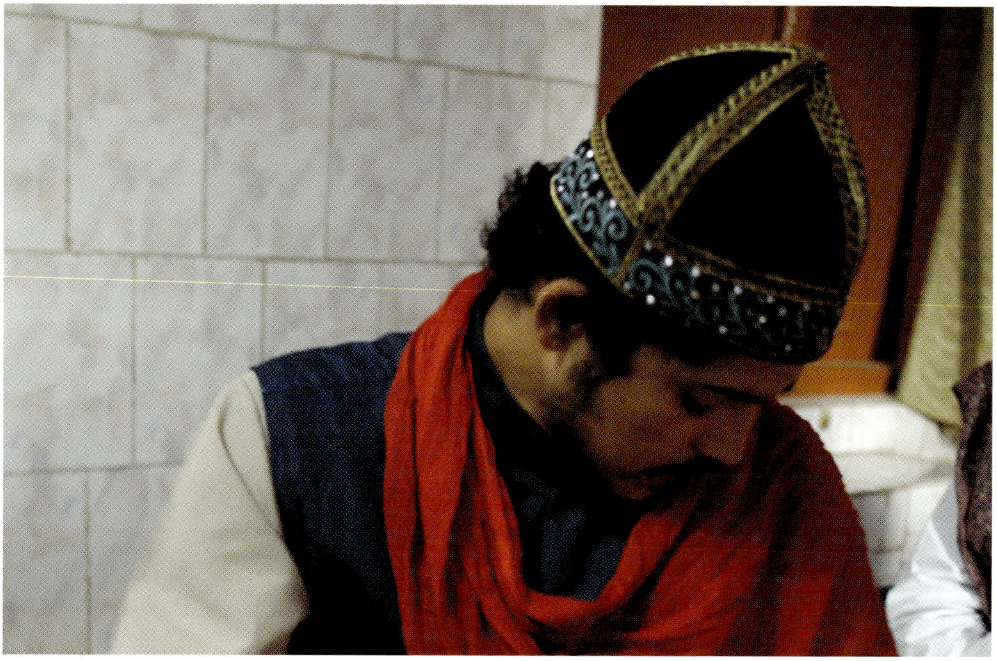

Shah Syed Hasnain Baqai in prayer,
Safipur, 2016

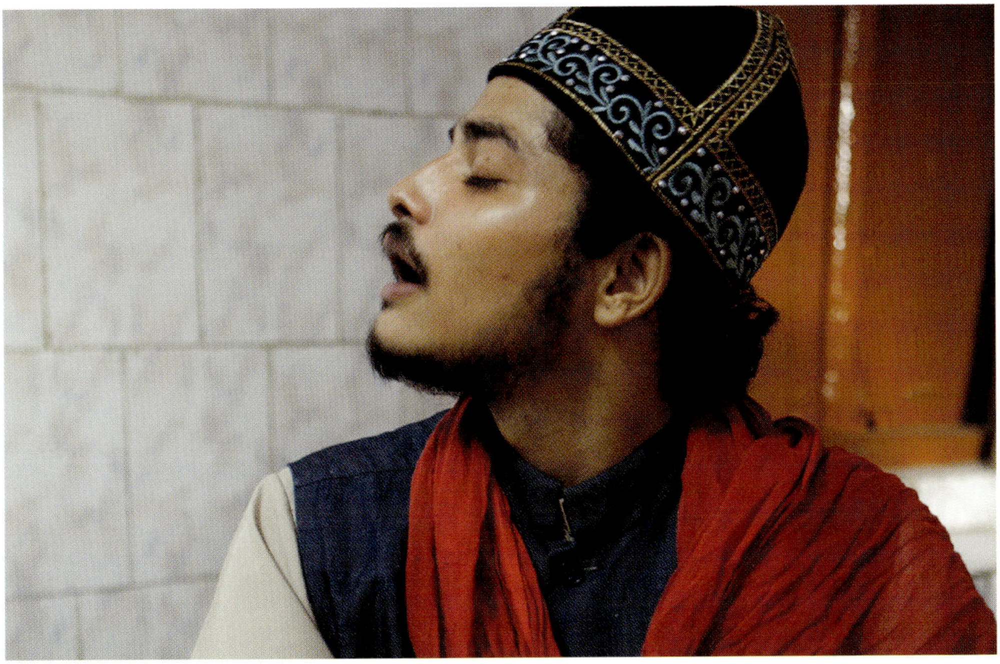

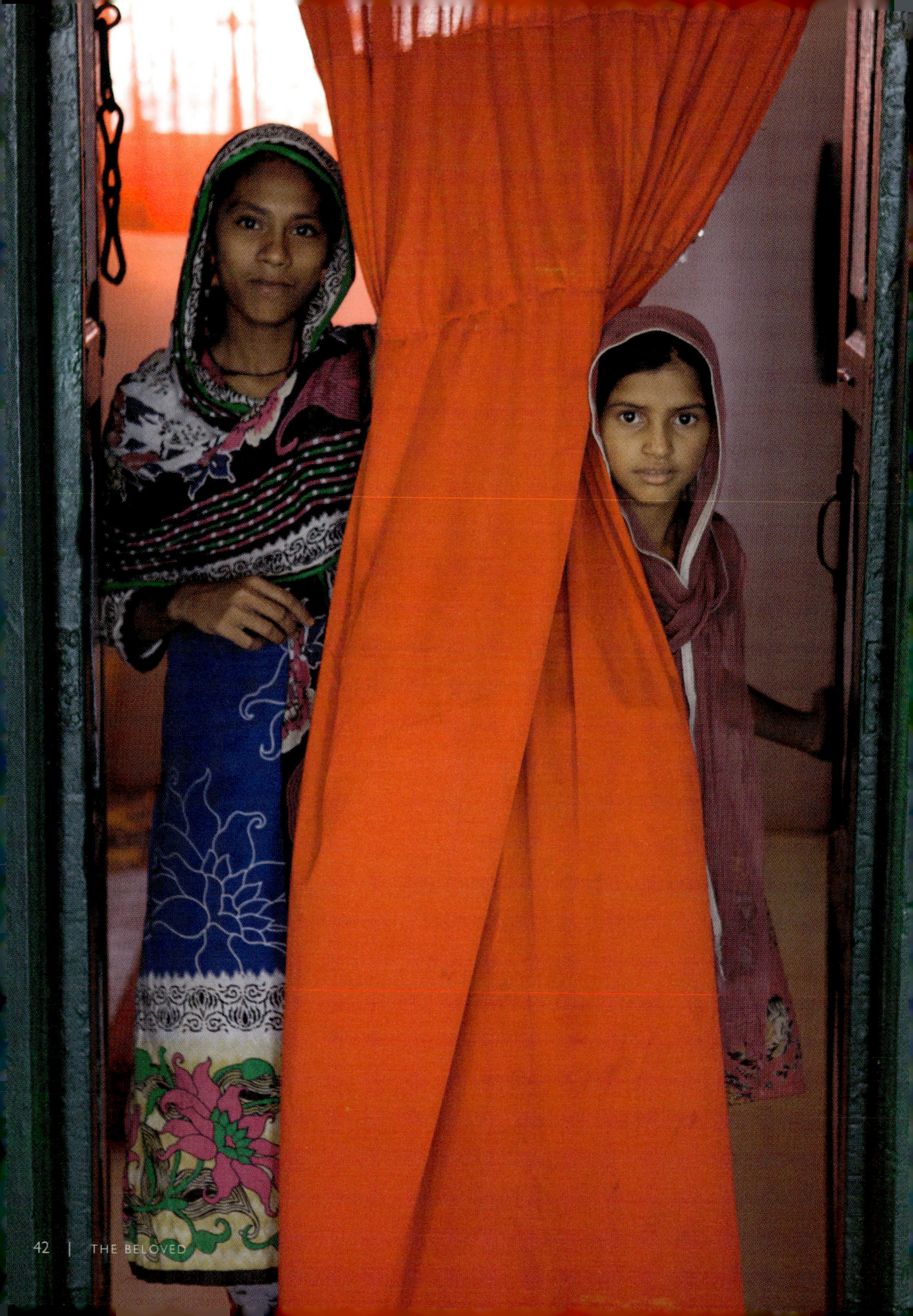

Safipur, 2016

RETREAT

I did not go to the mountains to seek out yogis, as I did not want to disturb them in their retreat, hence, most of my photographs were of practitioners passing through mainly urban places. There is something deeply comforting in knowing that you can practise your chosen way of being, of finding peace in the inner world, anywhere.

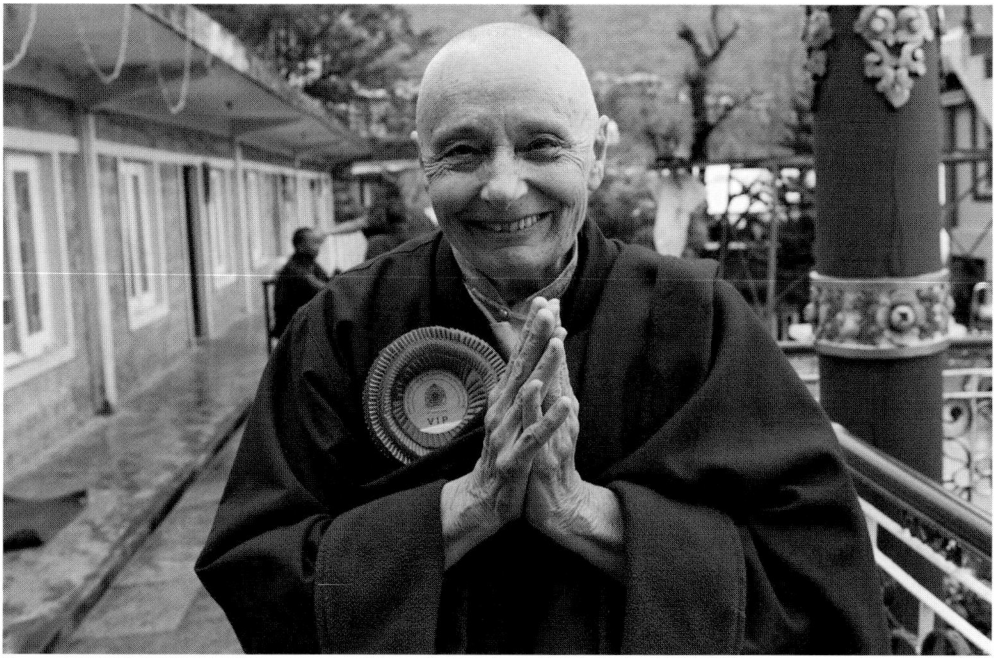

Jetsunma Tenzin Palmo,
Tashi Jong, Palampur, 2016

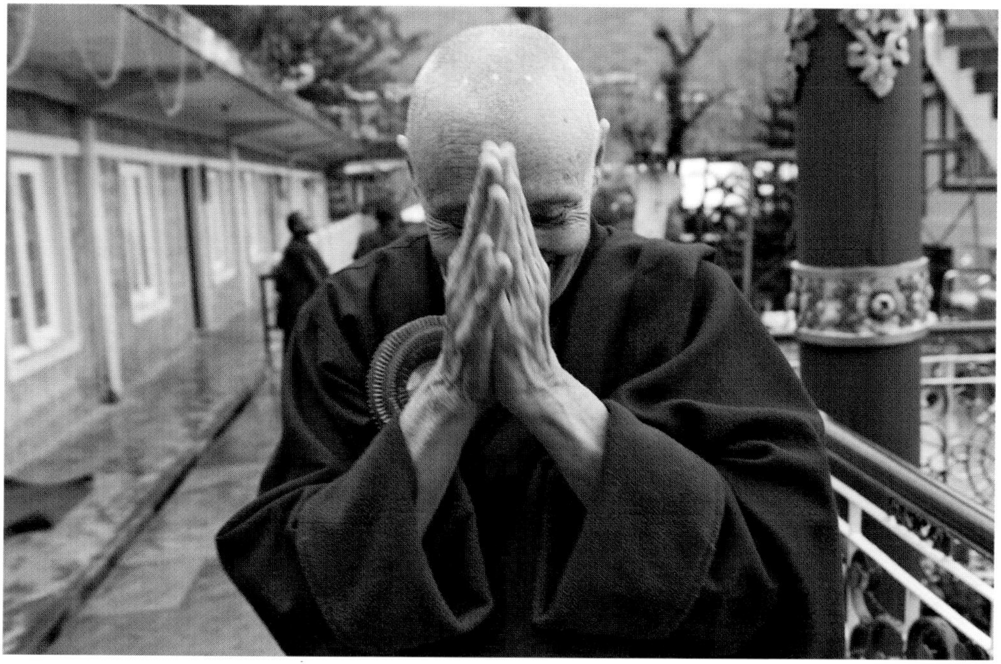

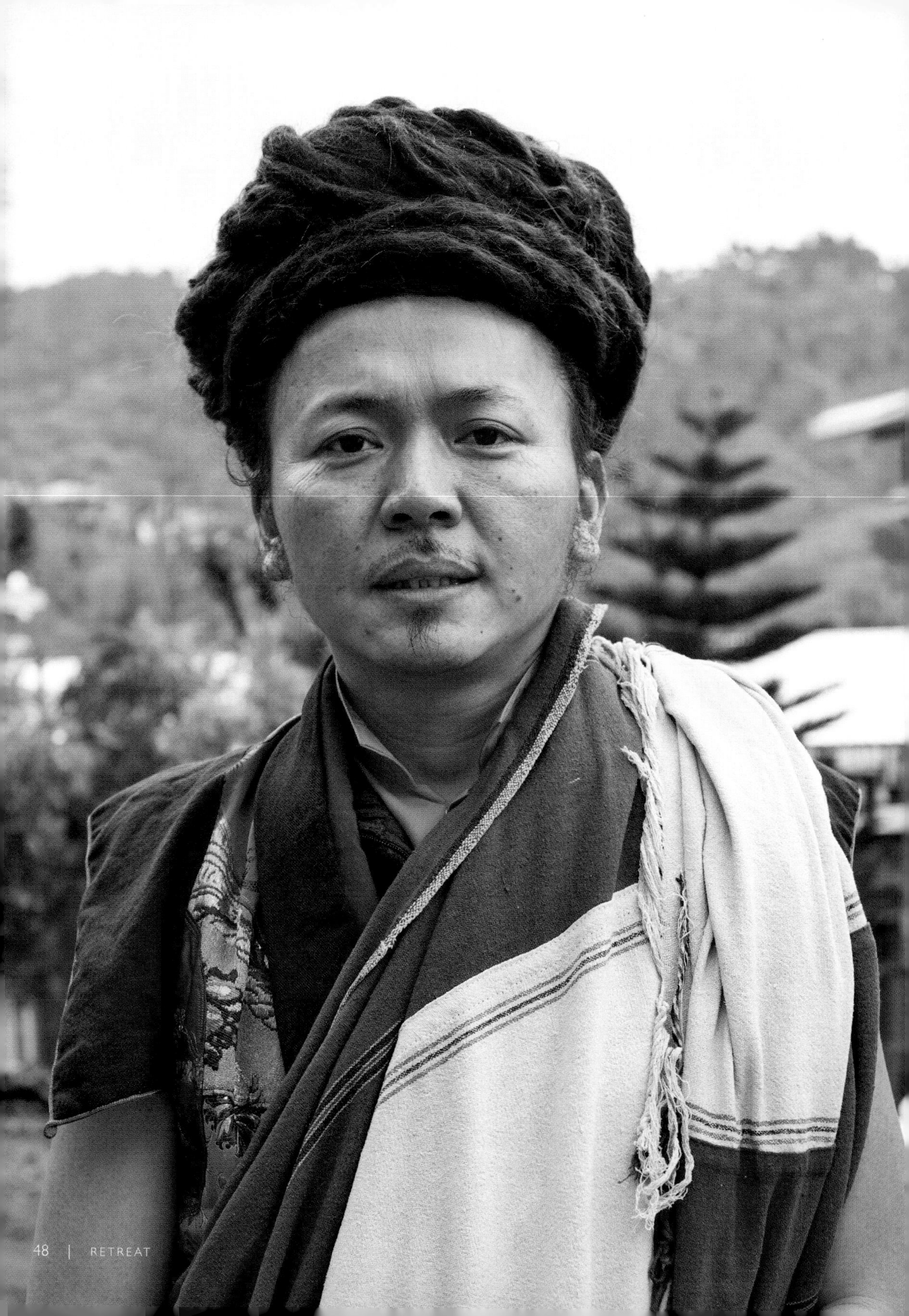

Tokden Drubgyu photographed after twelve years in retreat,
Tashi Jong, Palampur, 2016

Gelong Kalsang Tenzin recently reached Bodh Gaya from Tibet doing prostrations for the entire length of his three-year and six-month journey, Sarnath International Nyingma Institute, 2016

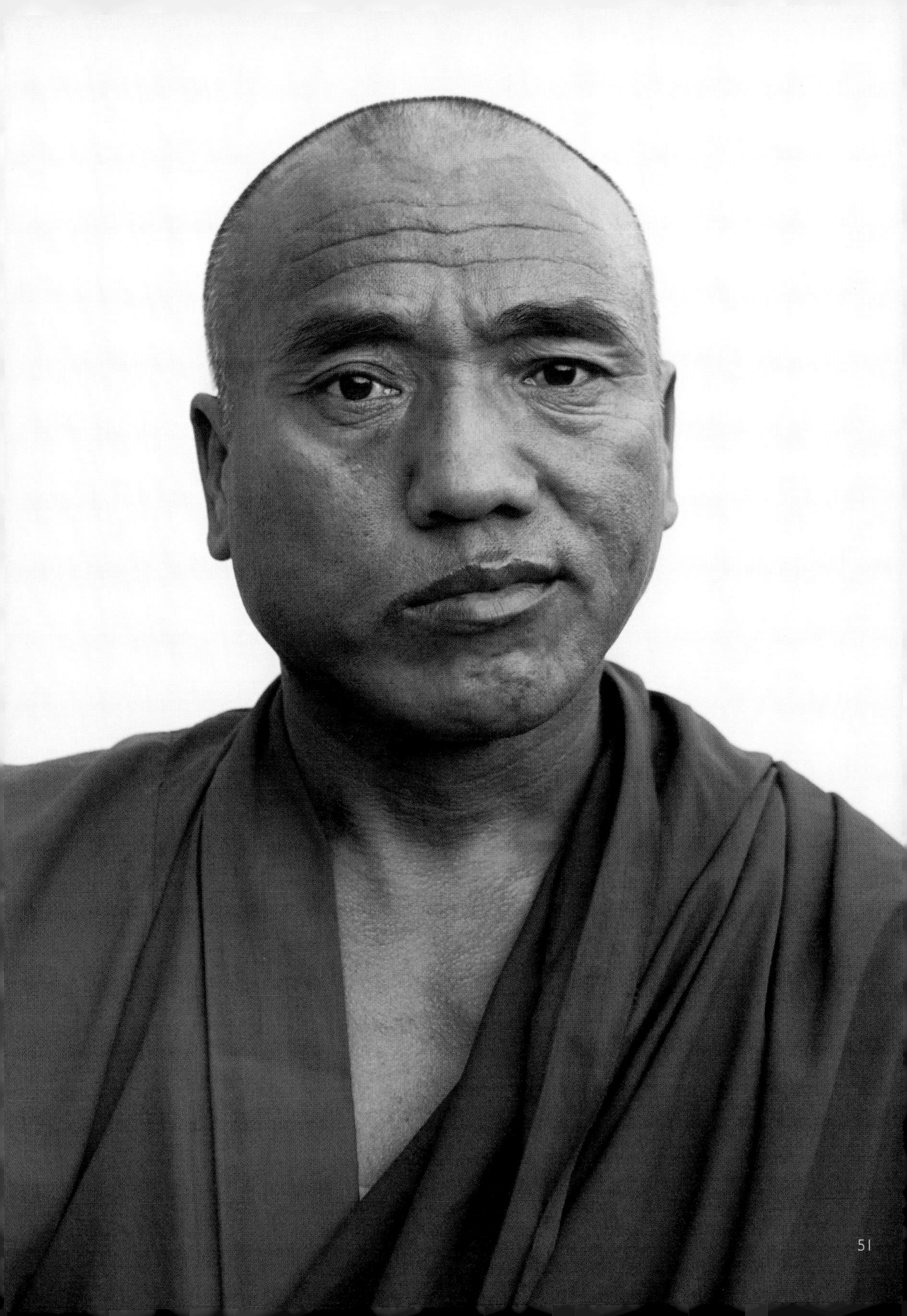

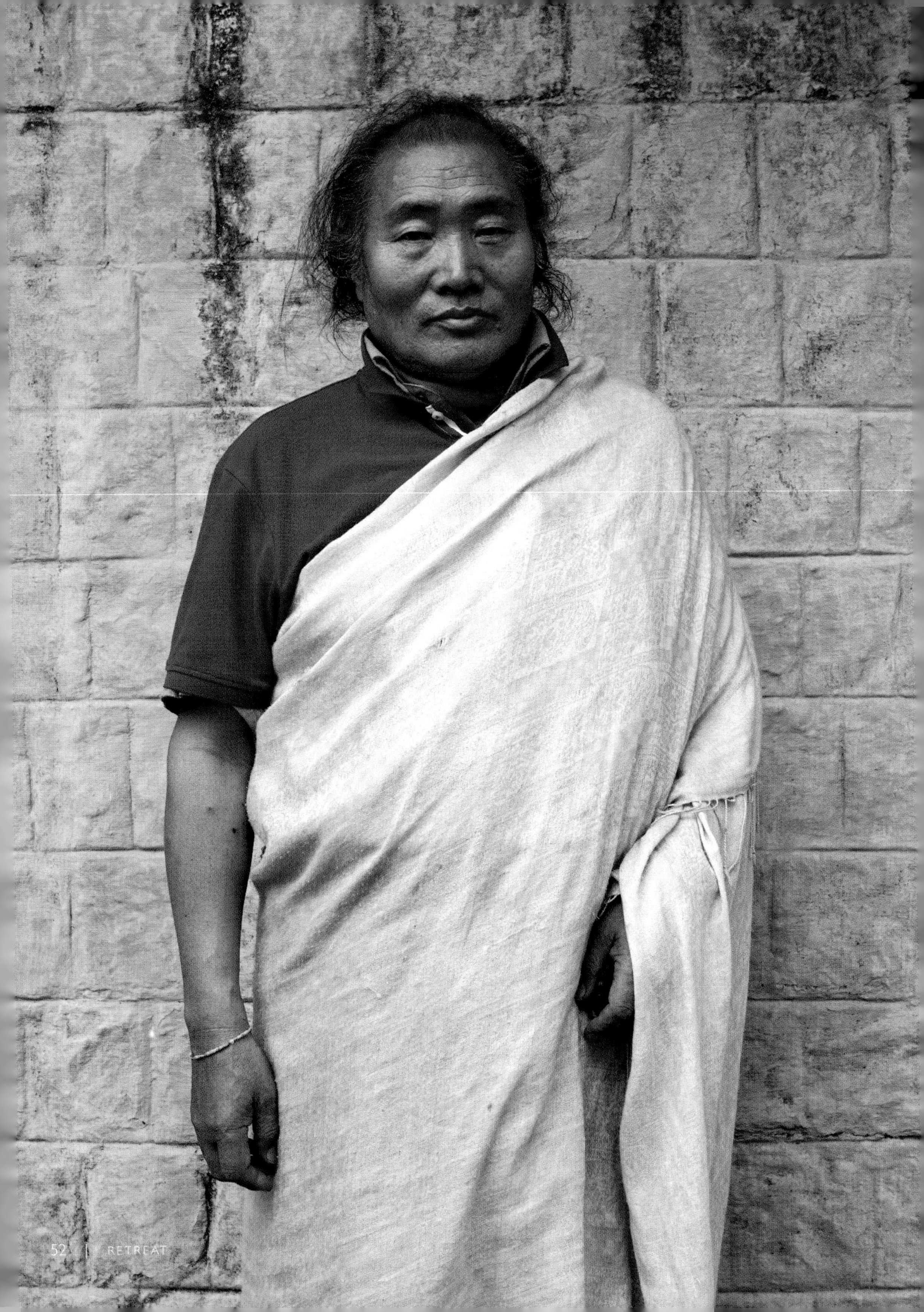

Tersi Osal Dorje Rinpoche,
Dalai Lama's Residence, Himachal Pradesh, 2015

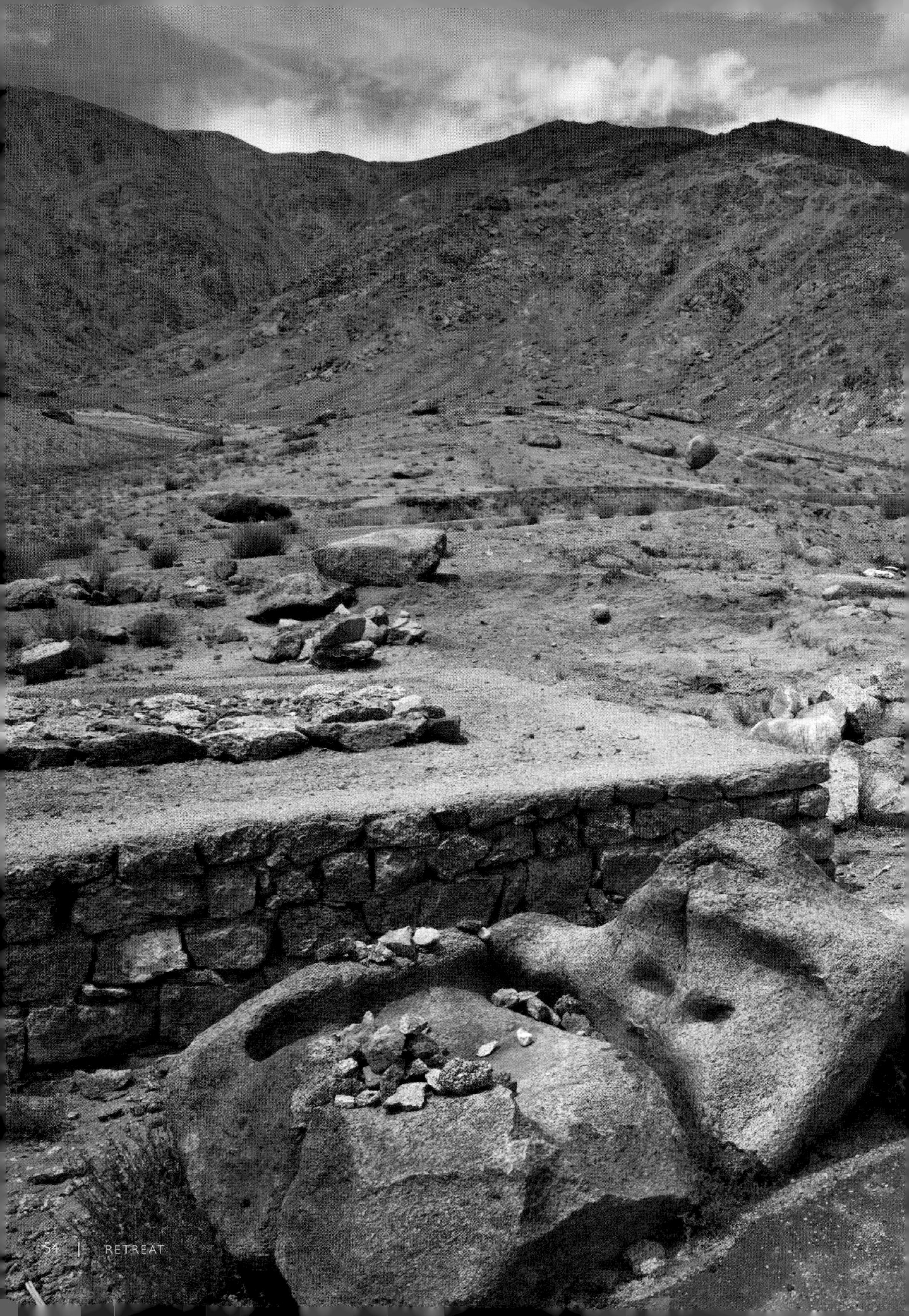

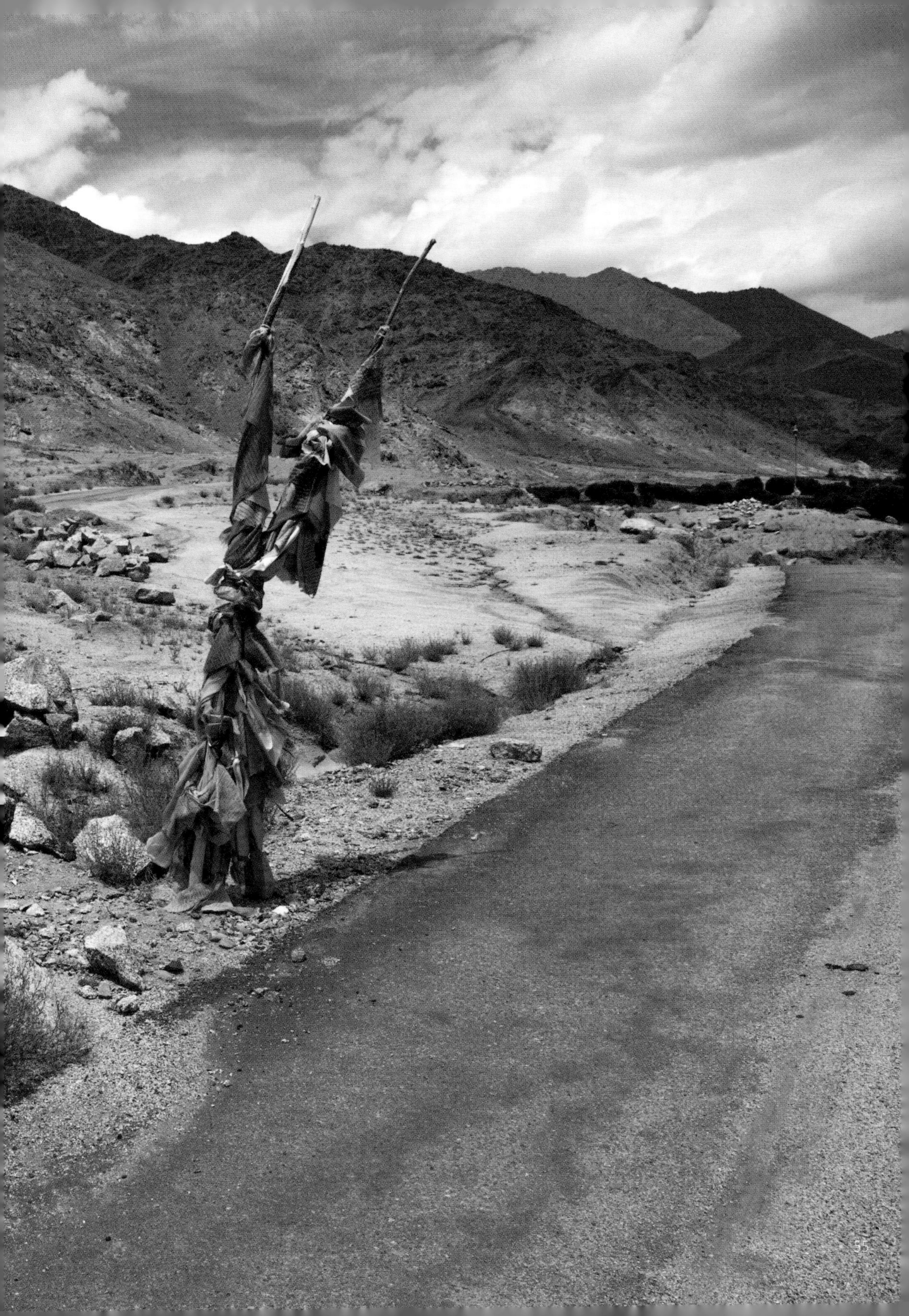

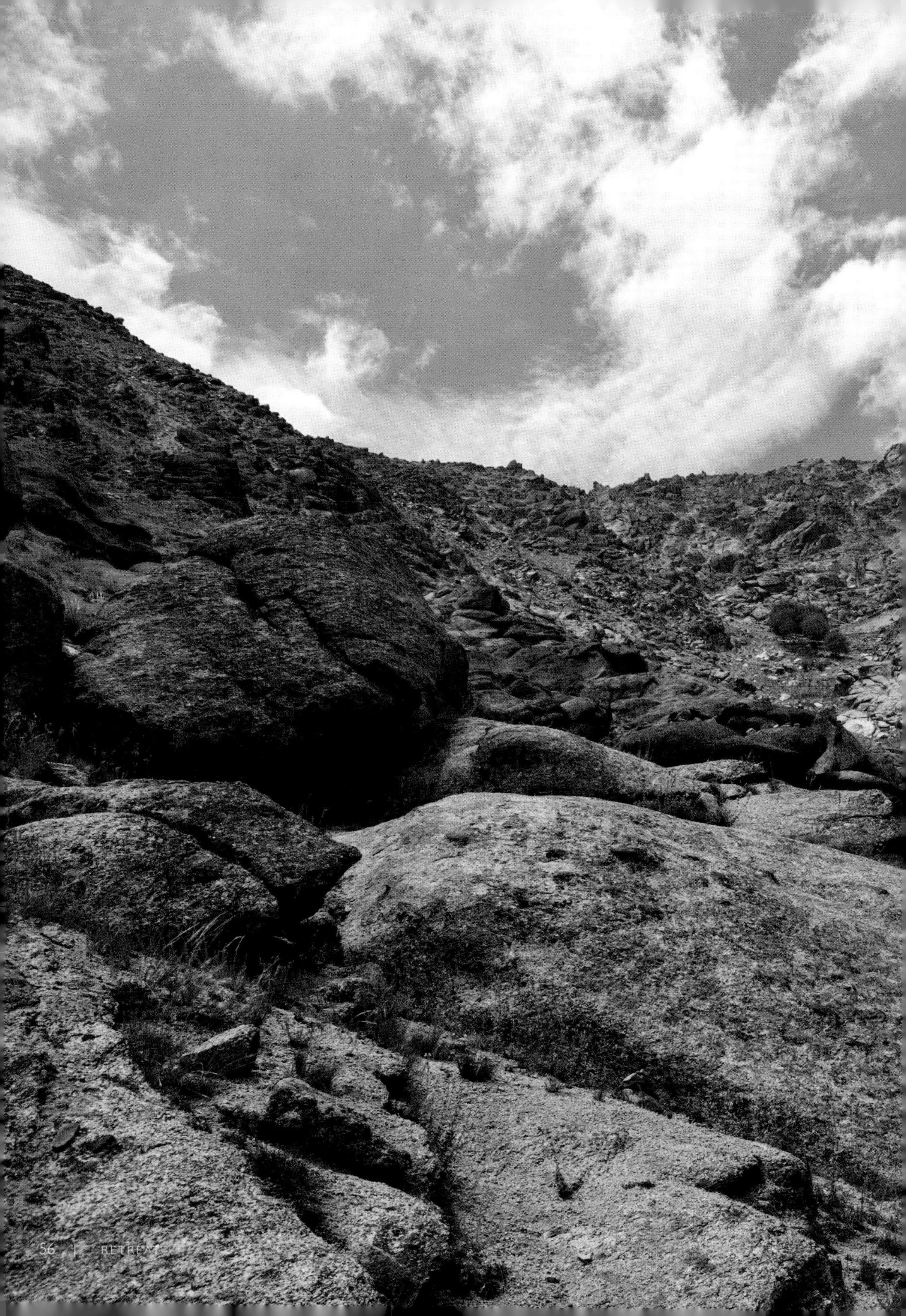

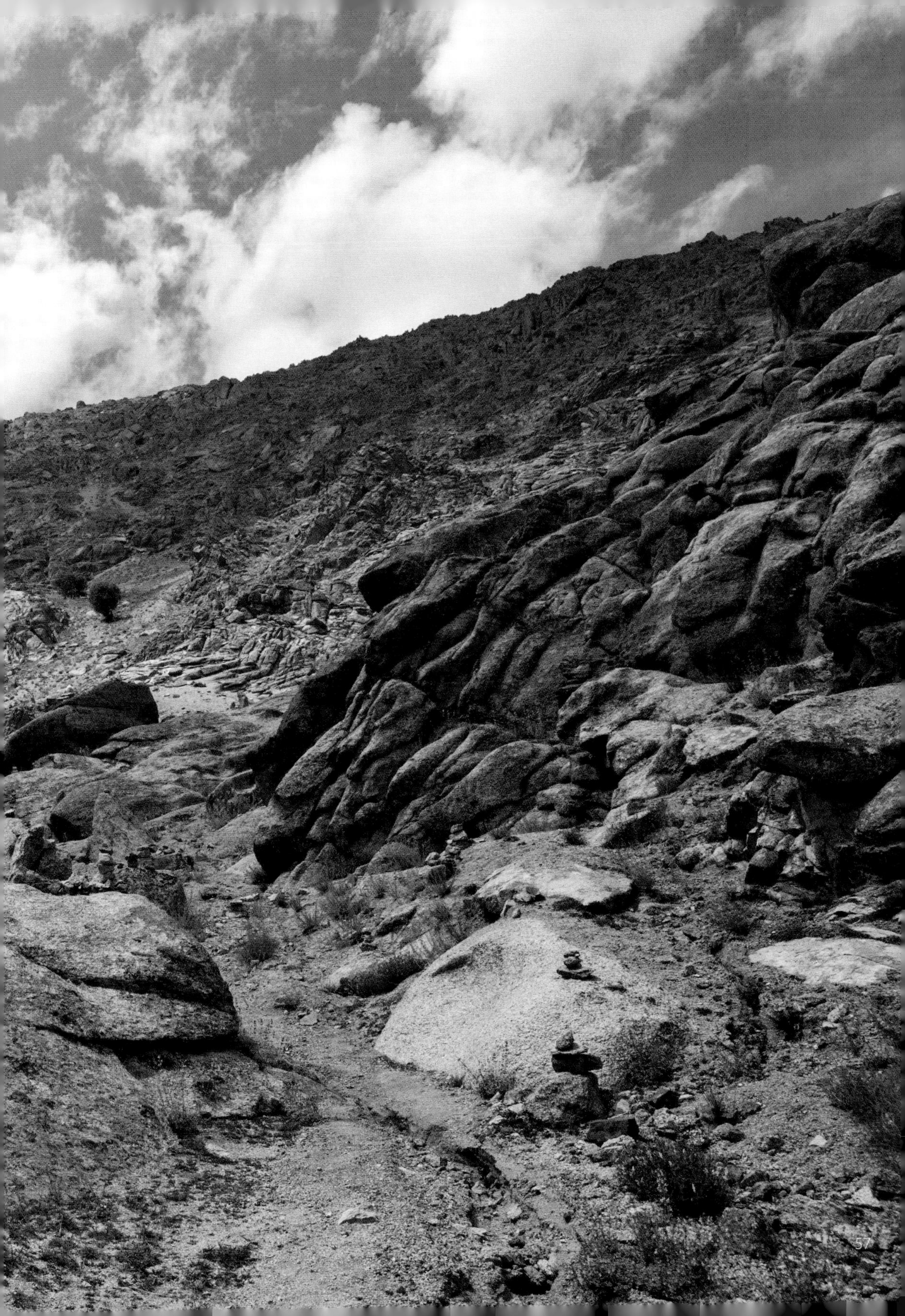

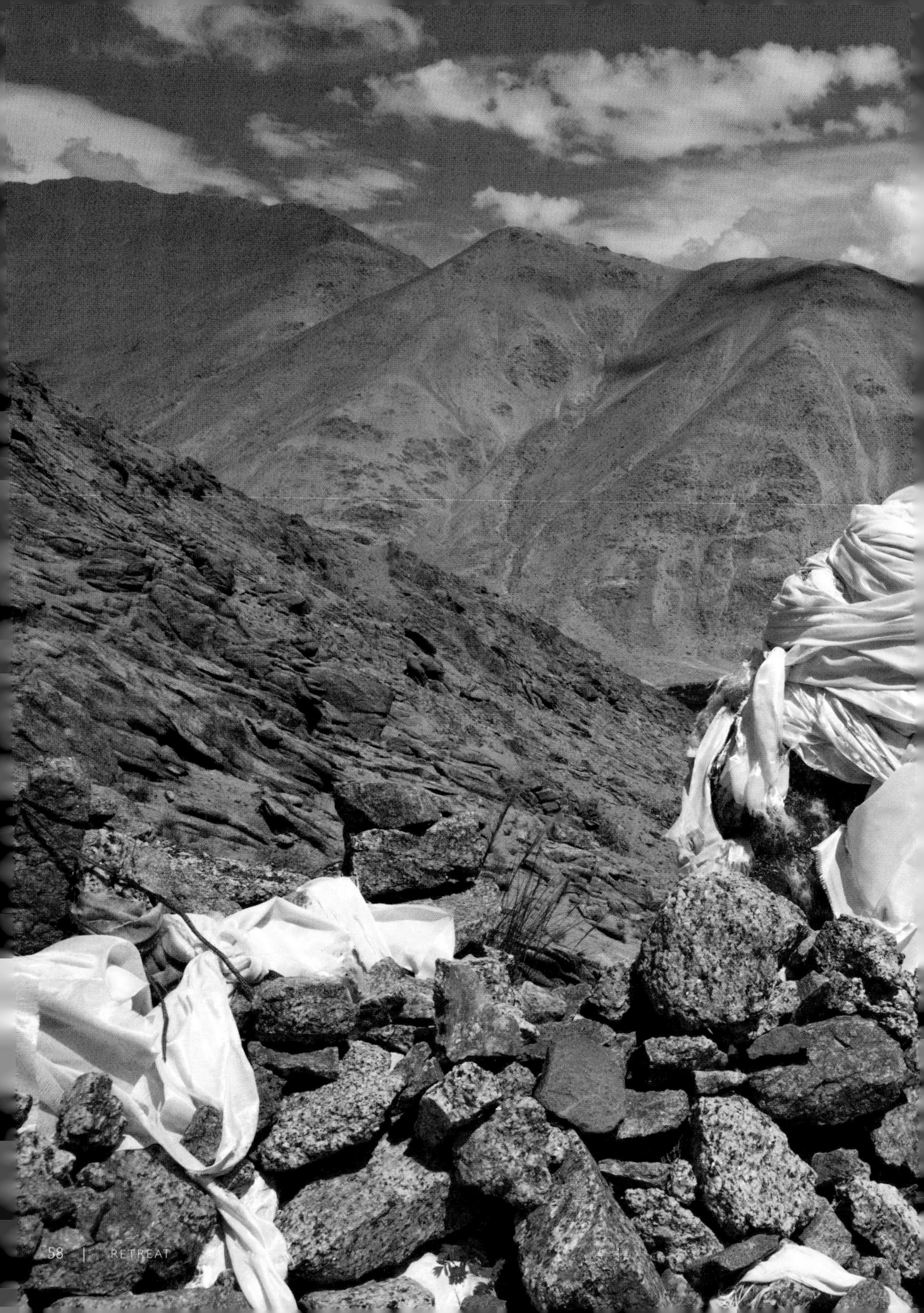

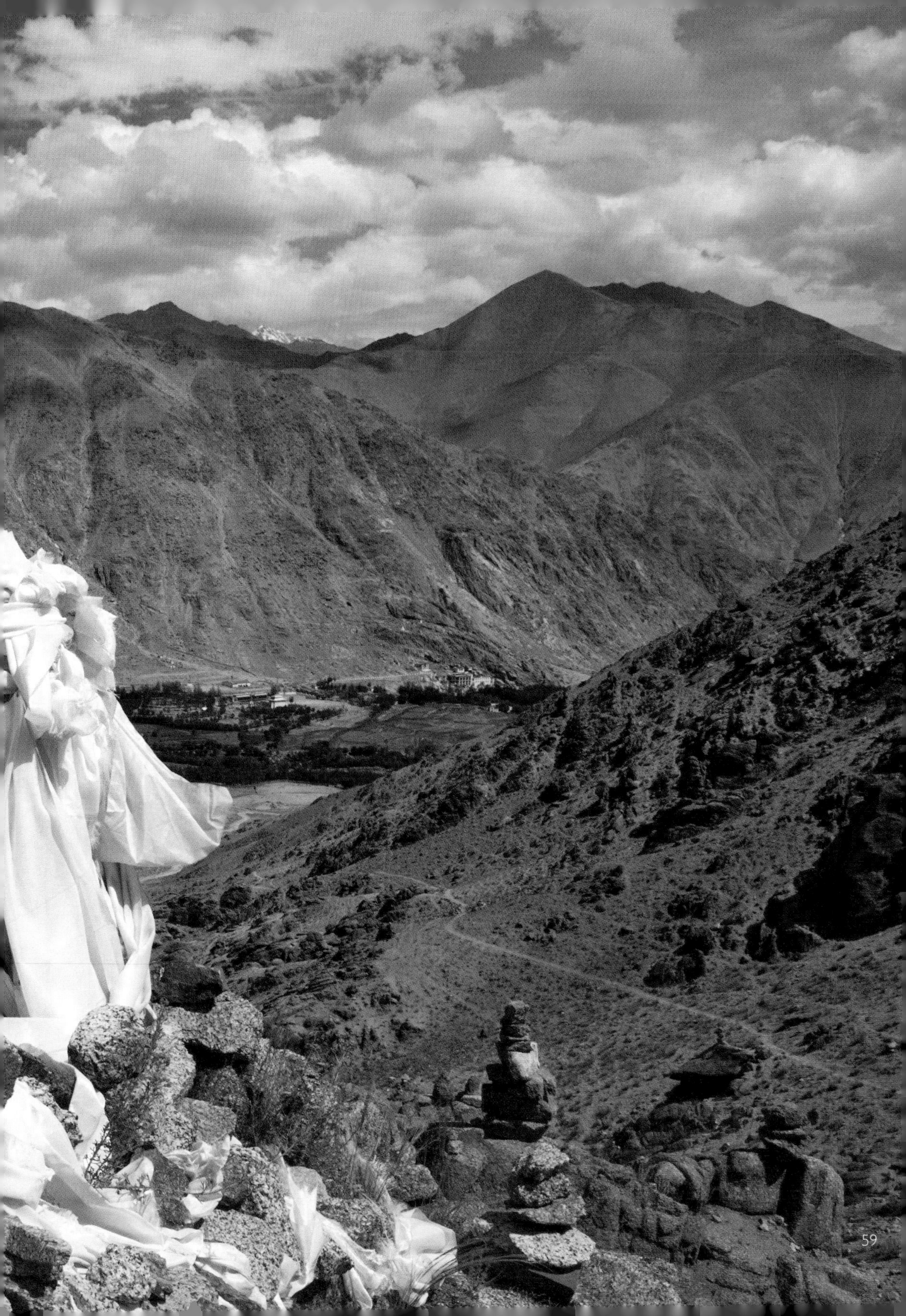

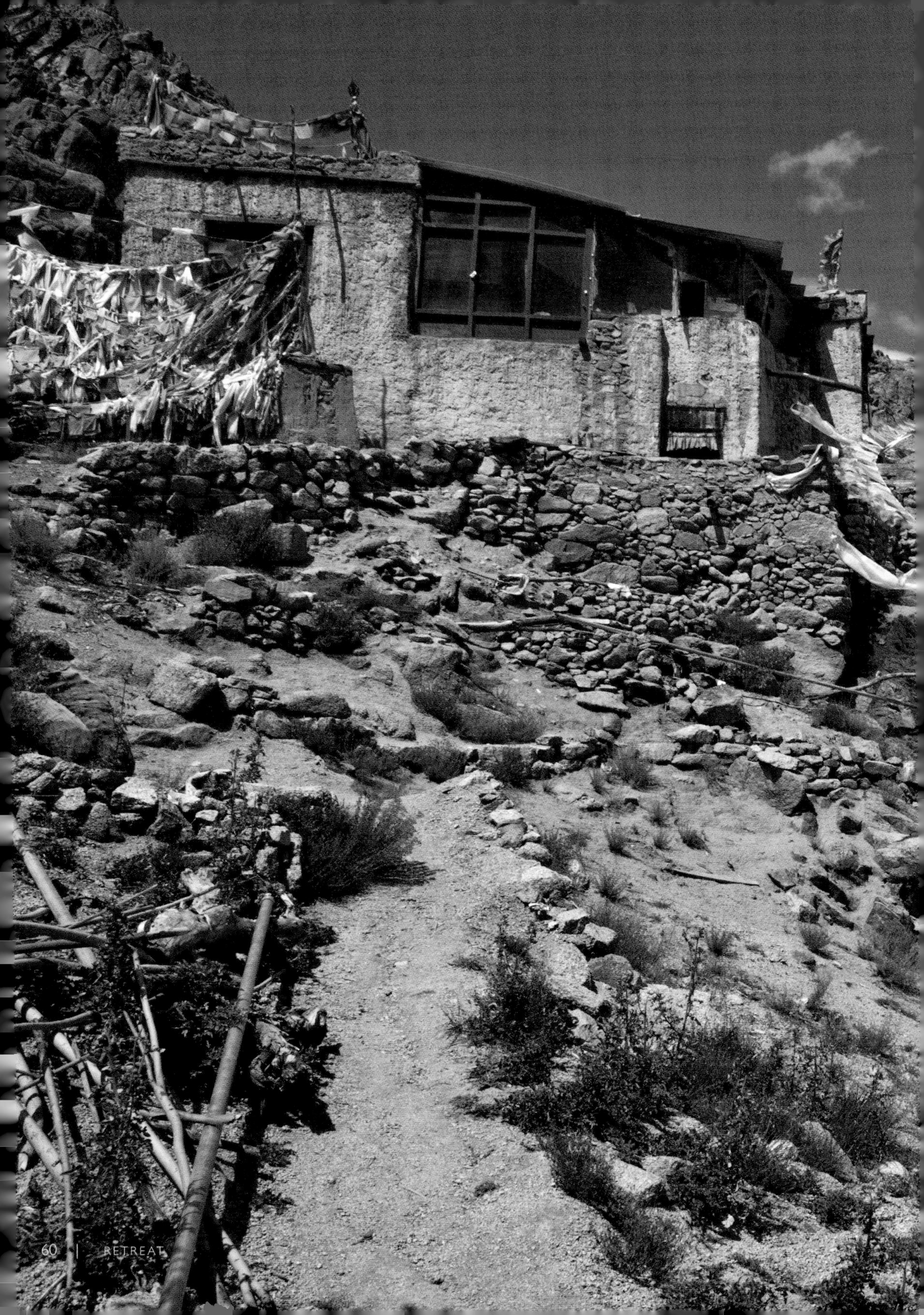

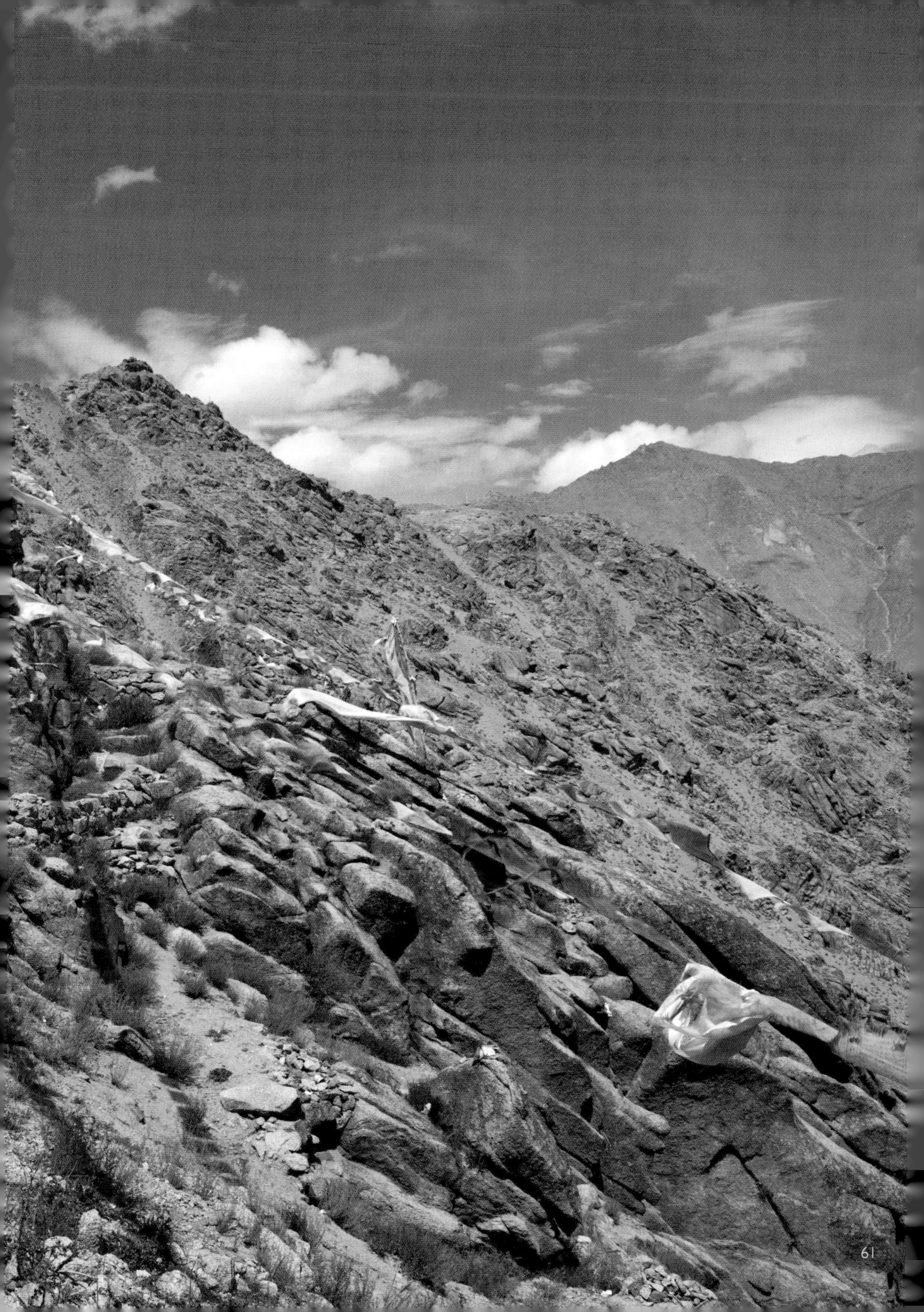

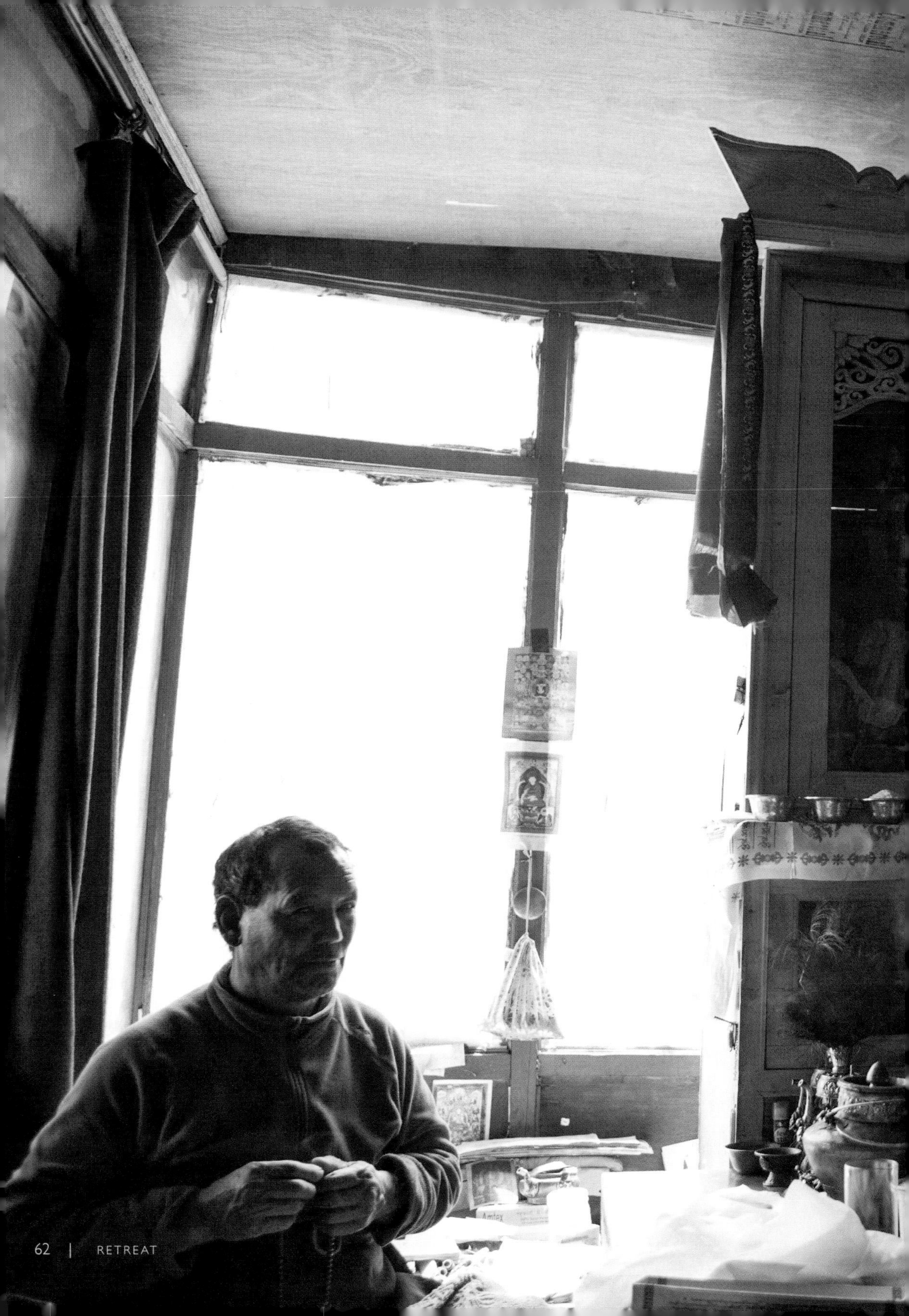

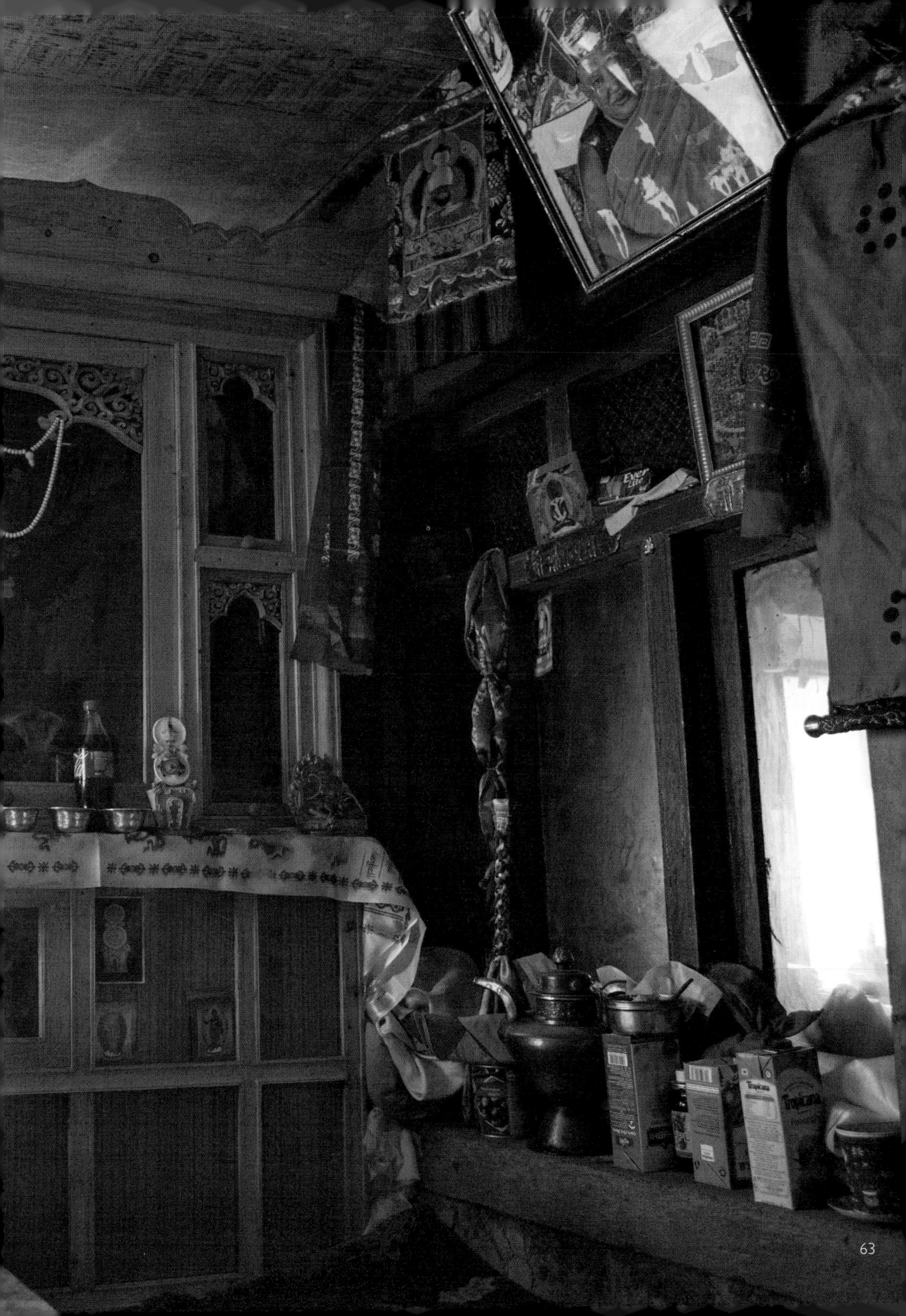
Ever Lite

Tokden Achos seated in his room,
Tashi Jong, Palampur, 2016

PAGES 54–59
Sakti, Ladakh, 2015

PAGES 60–61
The remote mountain retreat of Lama Shatup Raphel Rinpoche,
Ritod Padma Oling Mountain, Ladakh, 2015

PAGES 62–63
Lama Shatup Raphel Rinpoche inside his mountain retreat where
he has spent the last thirty years,
Ladakh, 2015

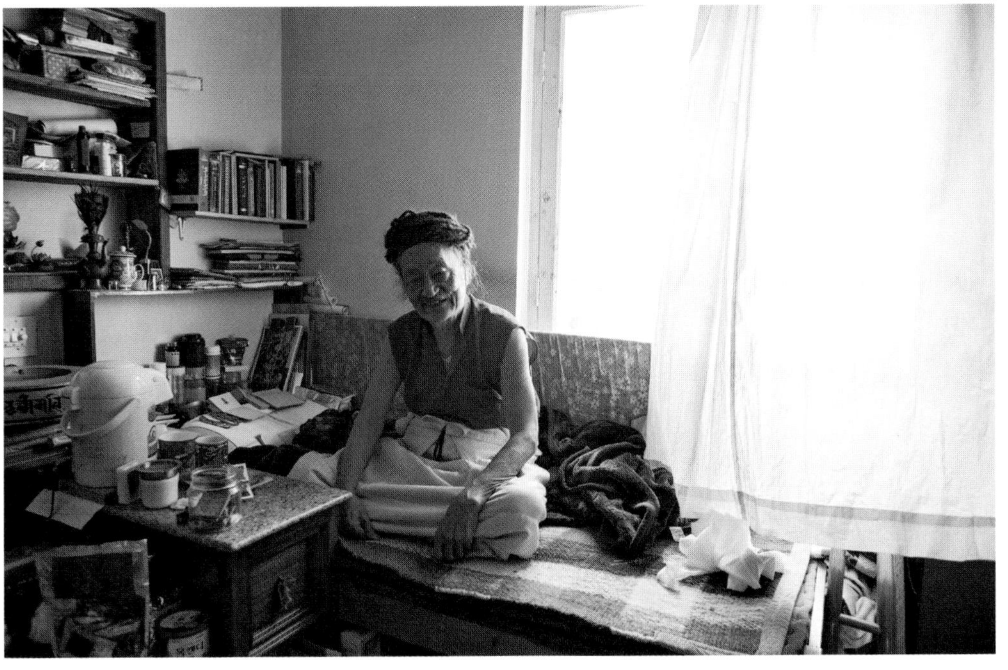

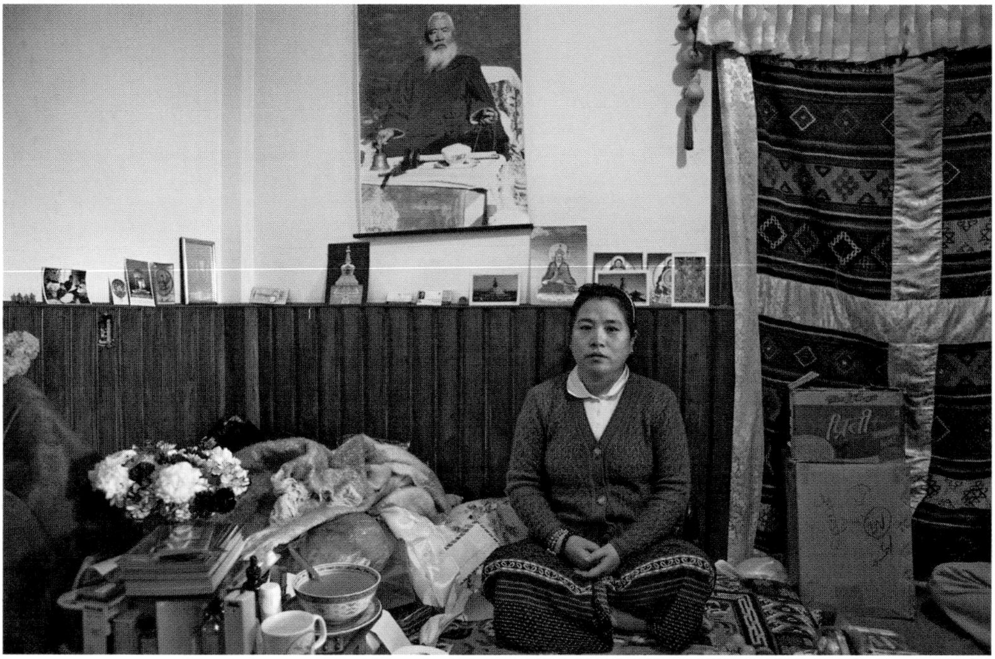

Semo Saraswati Lama, photographed on the 49th day of her father Chatral Rinpoche's funeral prayers,
Pharping, Nepal, 2016

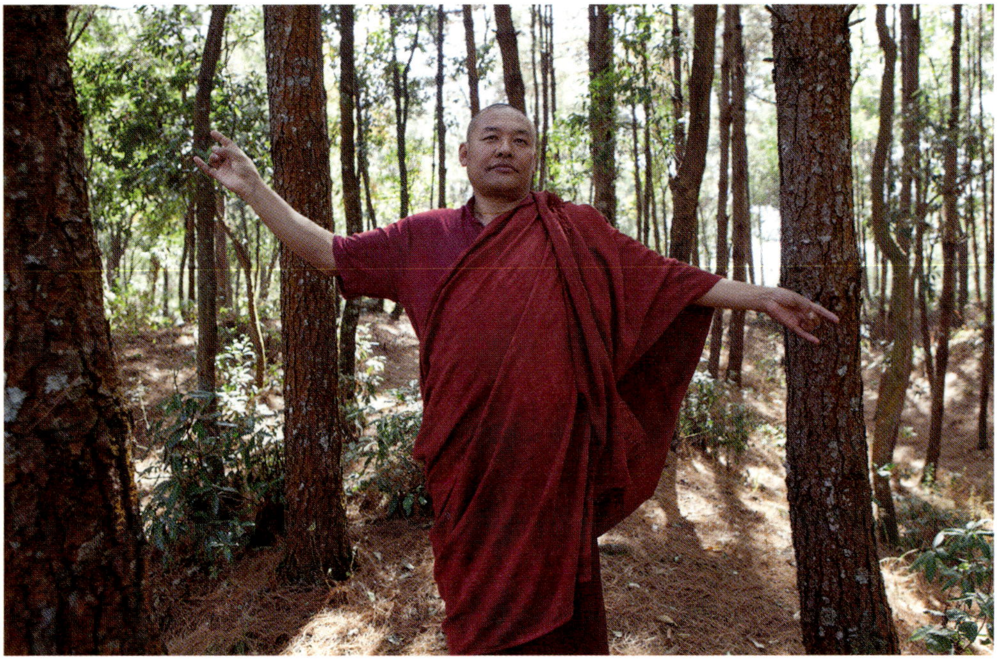

Lama Doshu demonstrating Tibetan Tsa Lung practices, a technique of healing movement that uses the body's wind energy to heal the subtle body, Pharping, Nepal, 2016

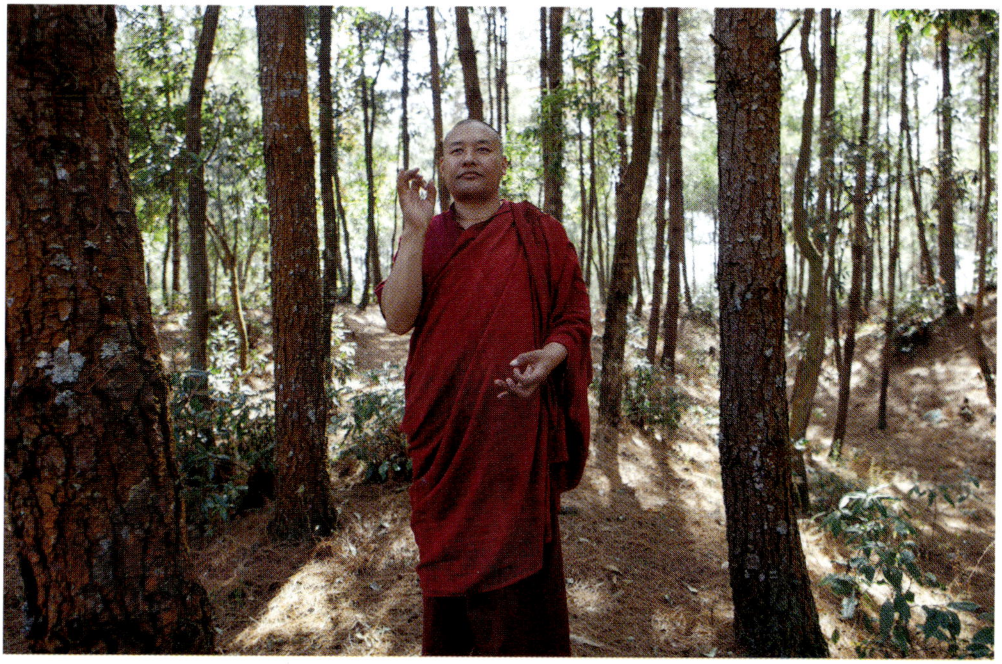

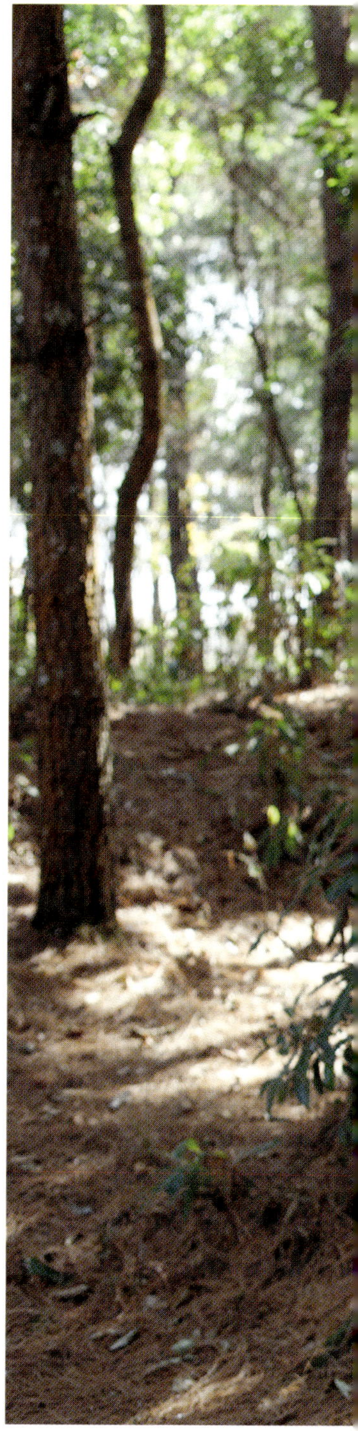

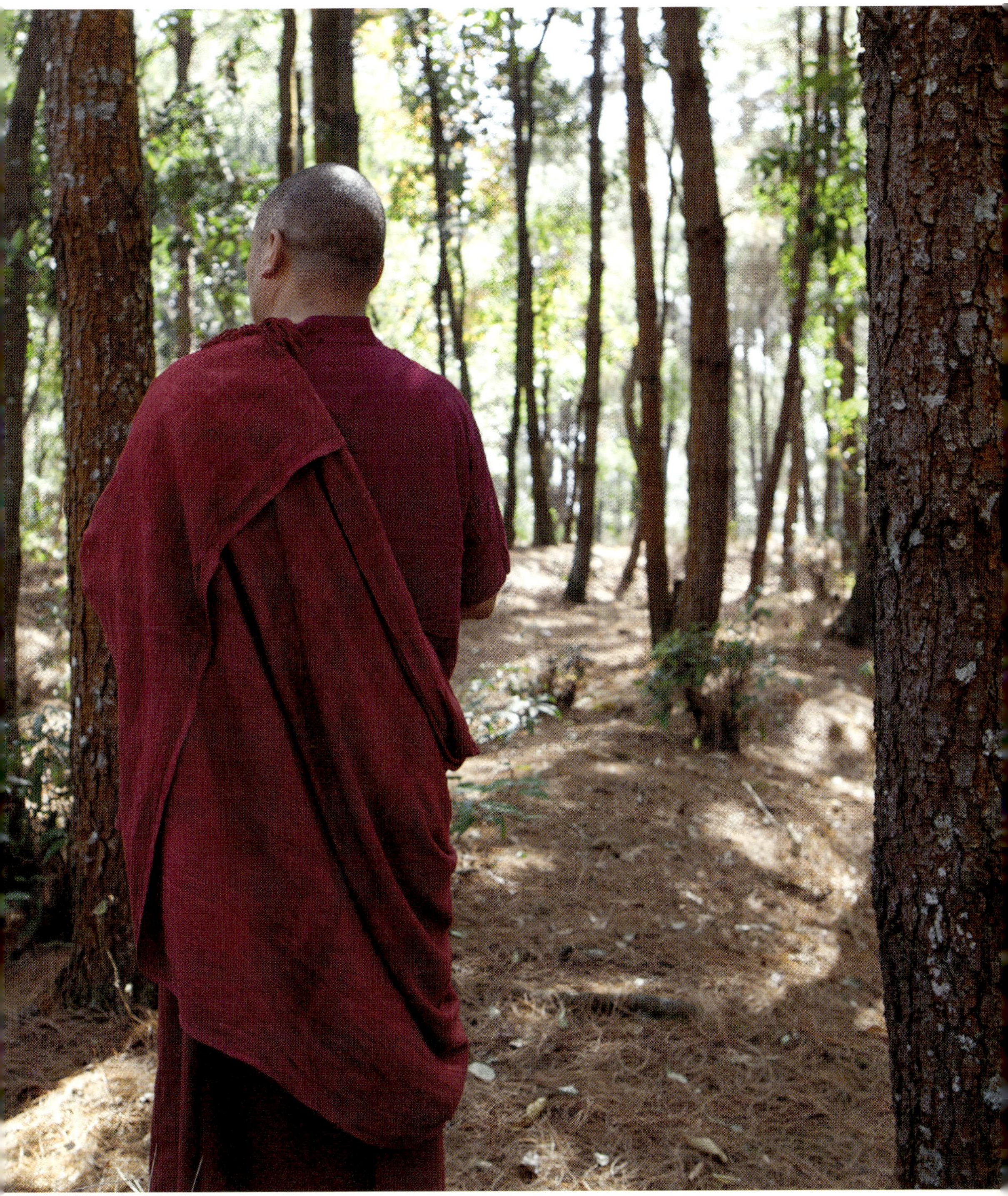

DEVOTION

In search of the divine, there are no scripted performers or performances, only spontaneous expressions of the leela. At the heart of all the traditions I encountered, devotion to the guru, to the teacher, to the divine, was the gateway to opening the heart.

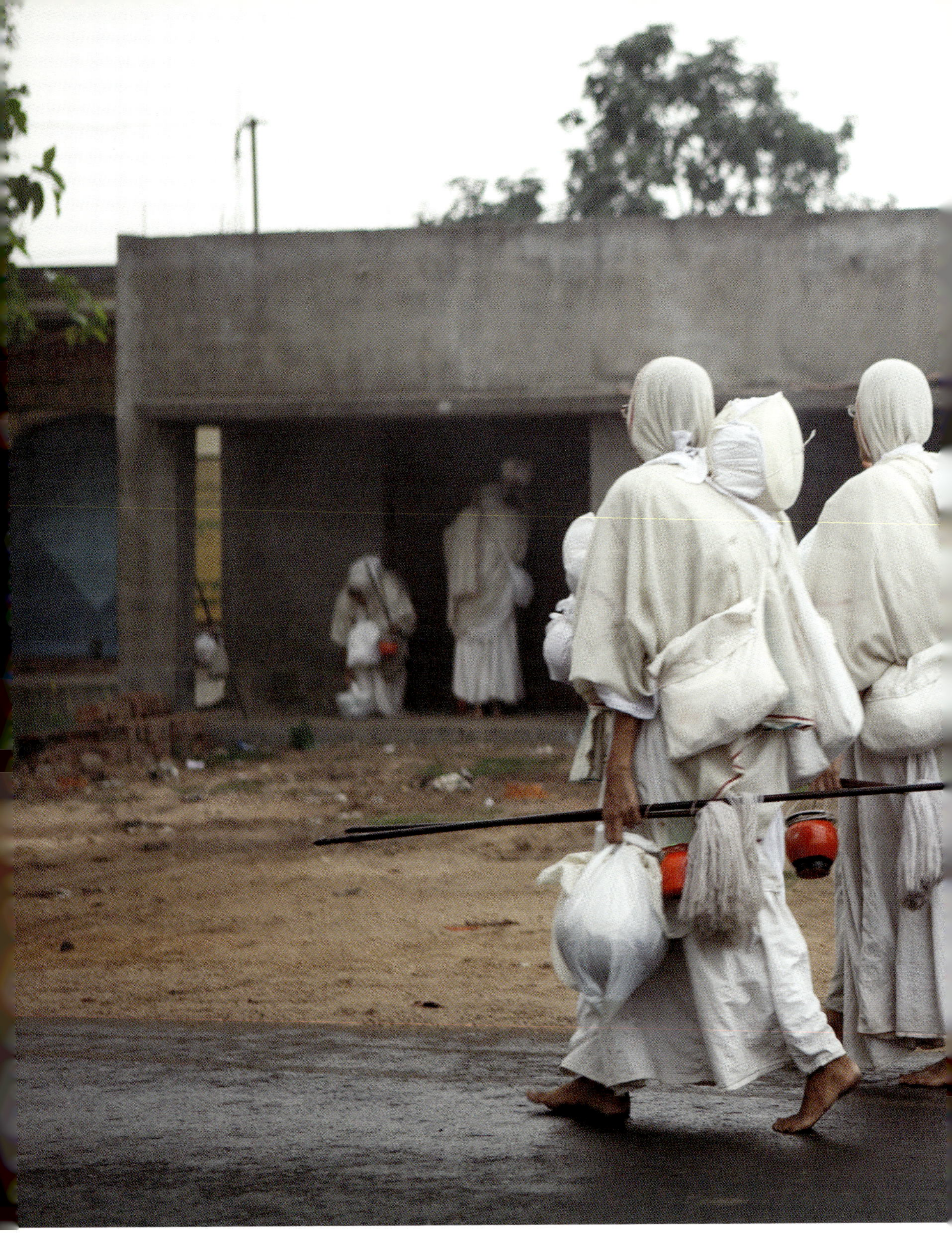

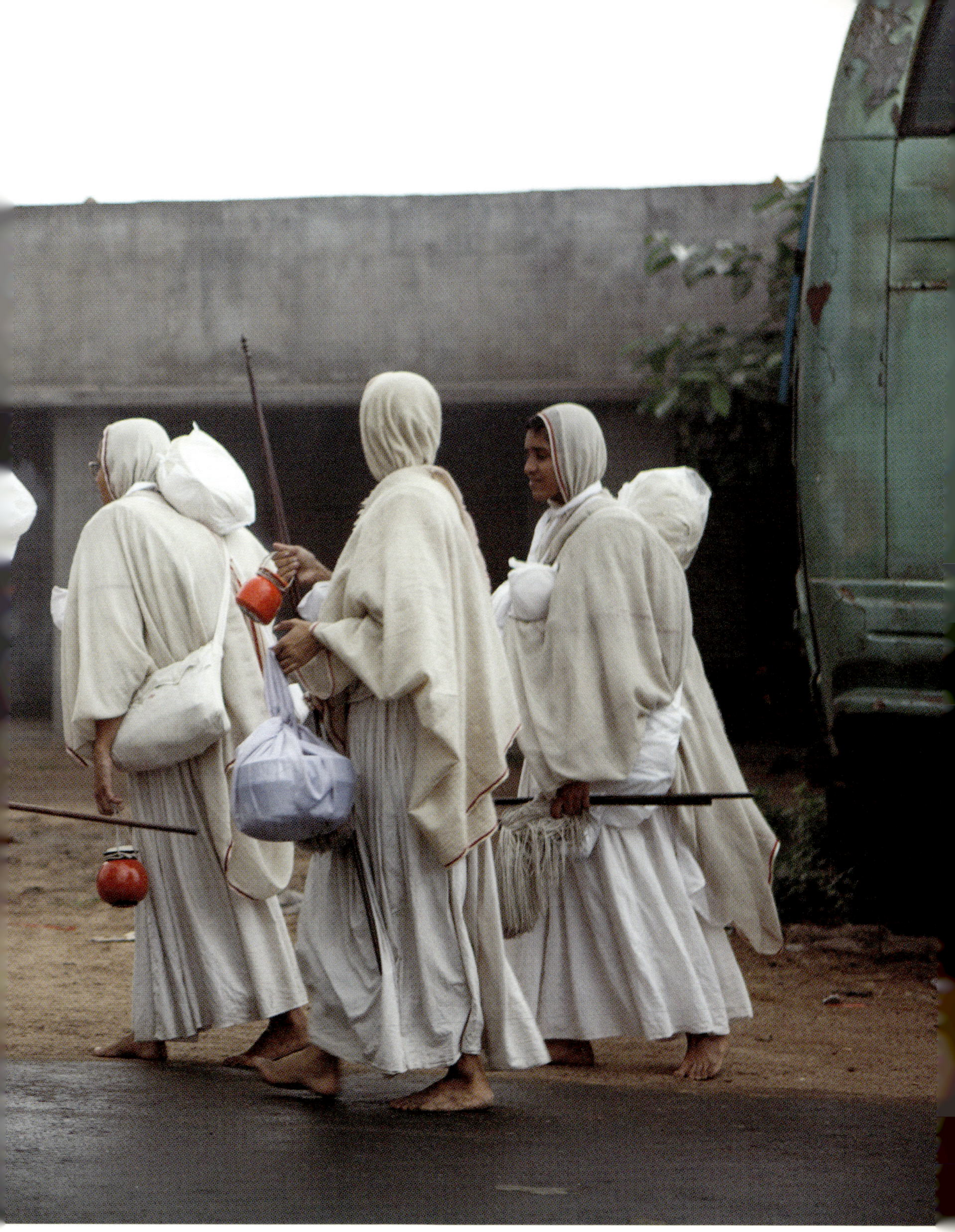

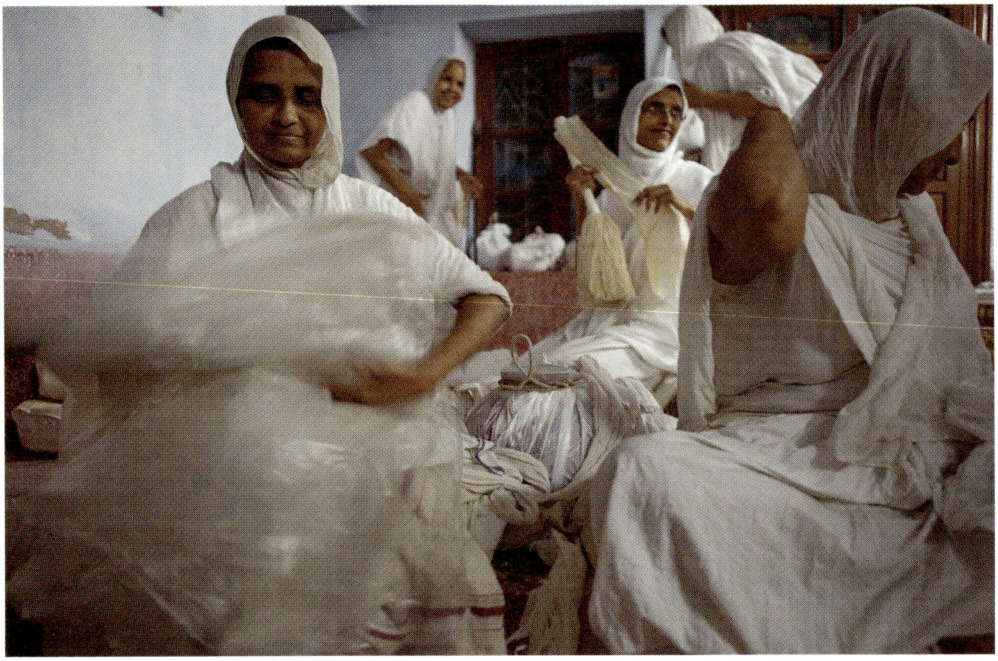

Swetamber Jain nuns unfolding layers of cloth and plastic wound tightly around their bodies, Jharkand, 2016

PAGES 74–75
Swetamber Jain nuns on Vihar, Jharkand, 2016

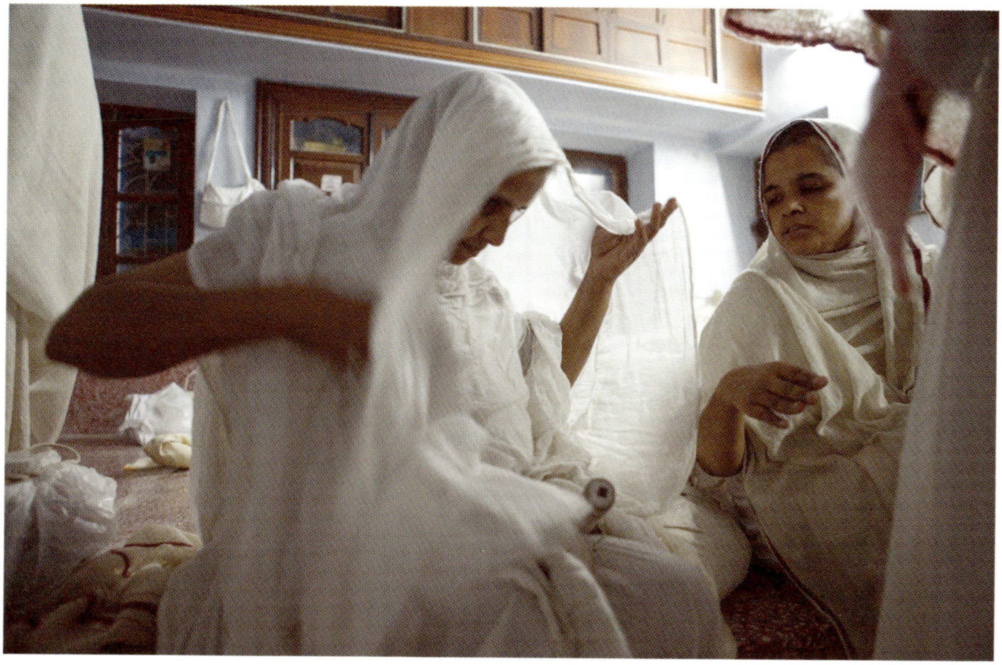

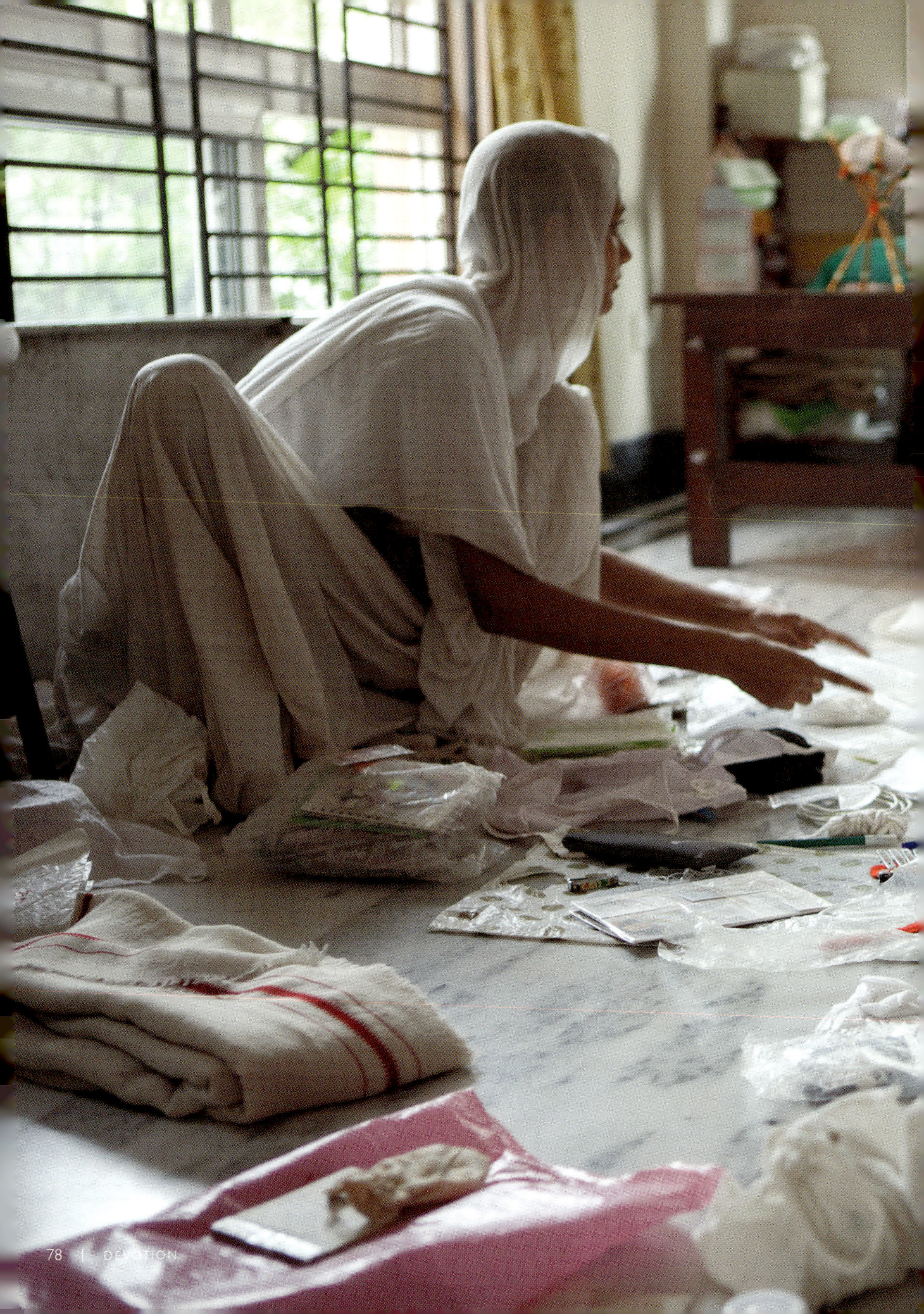

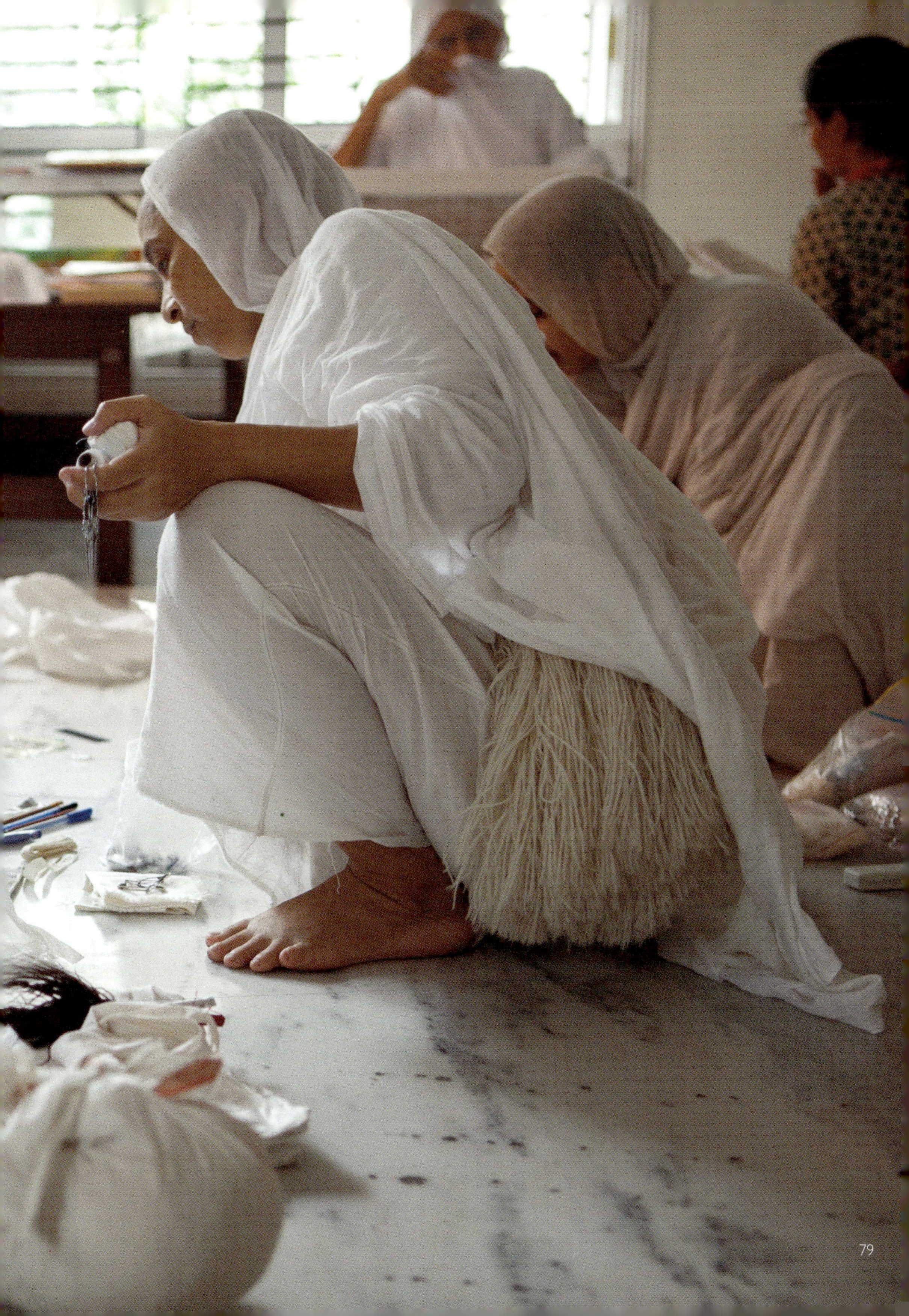

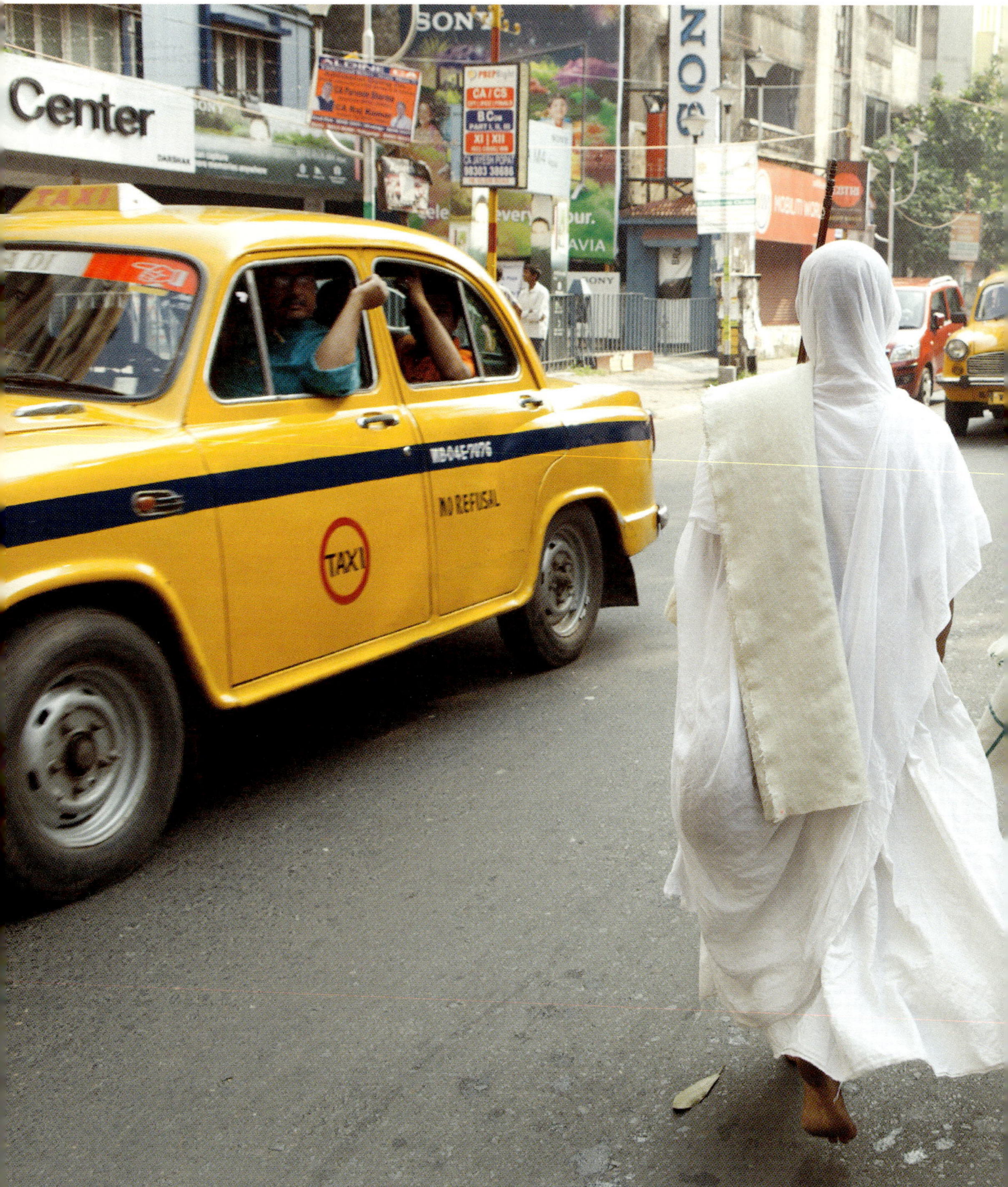
Center
SONY
CA / CS
TAXI
NO REFUSAL
TAXI

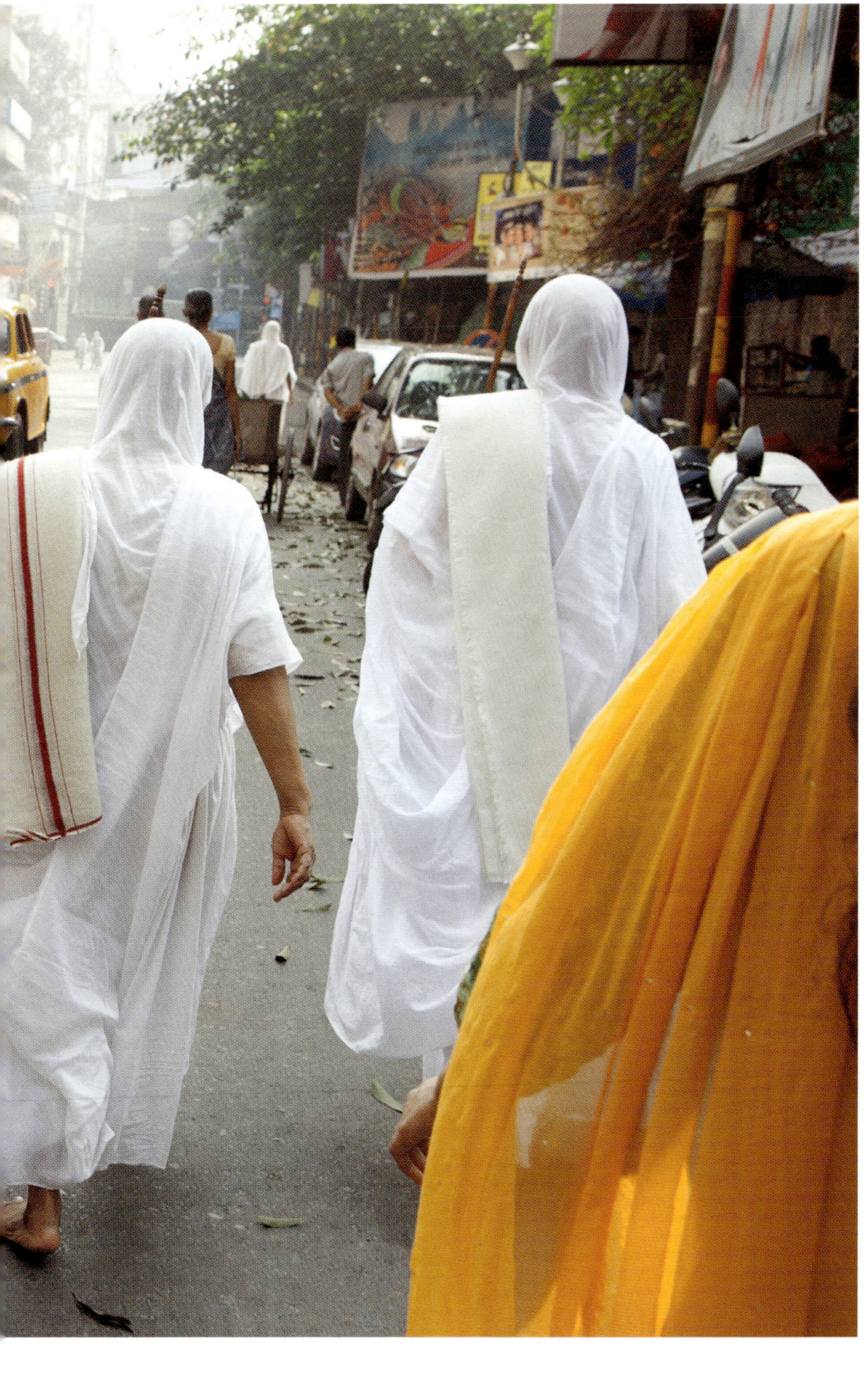

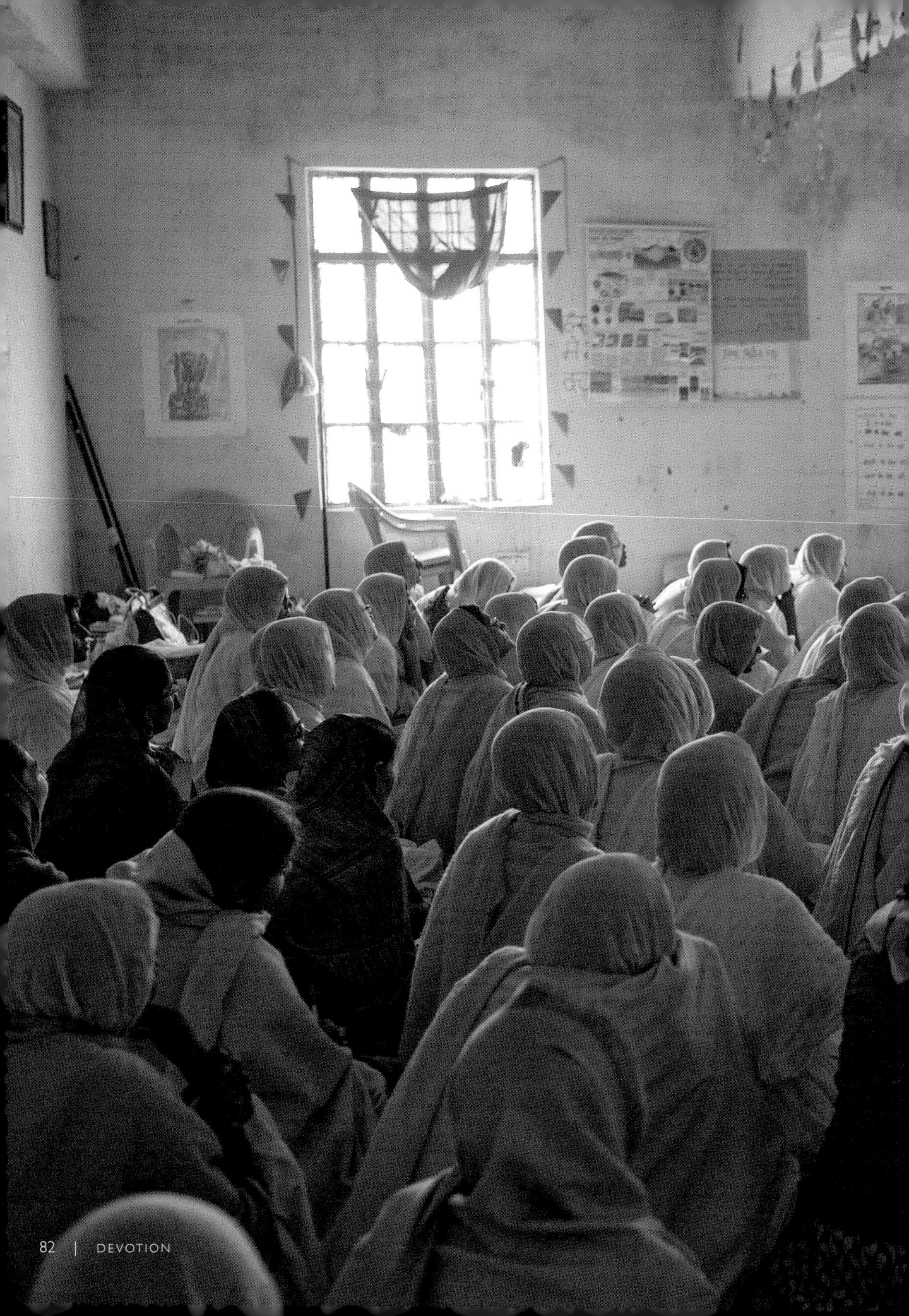

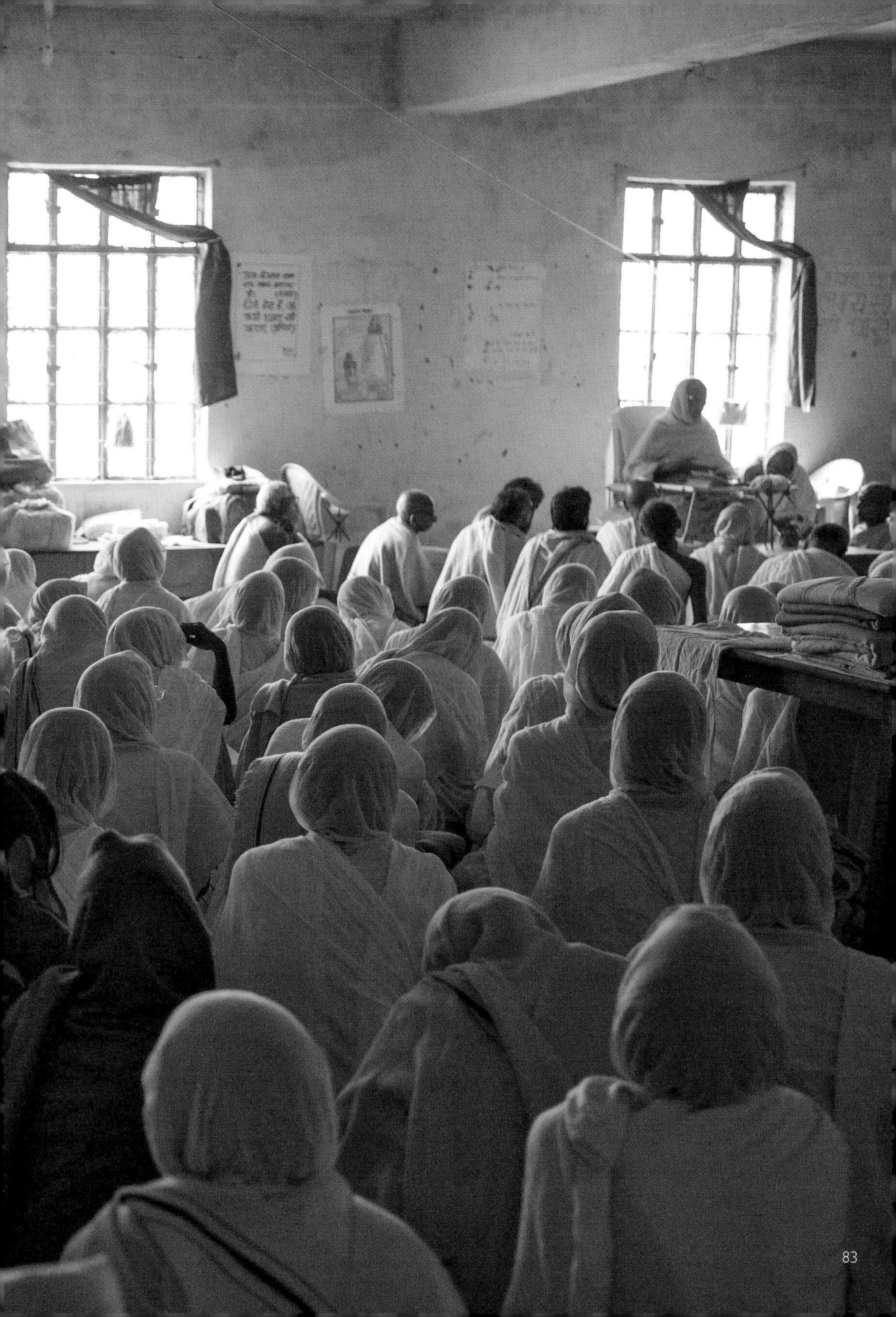

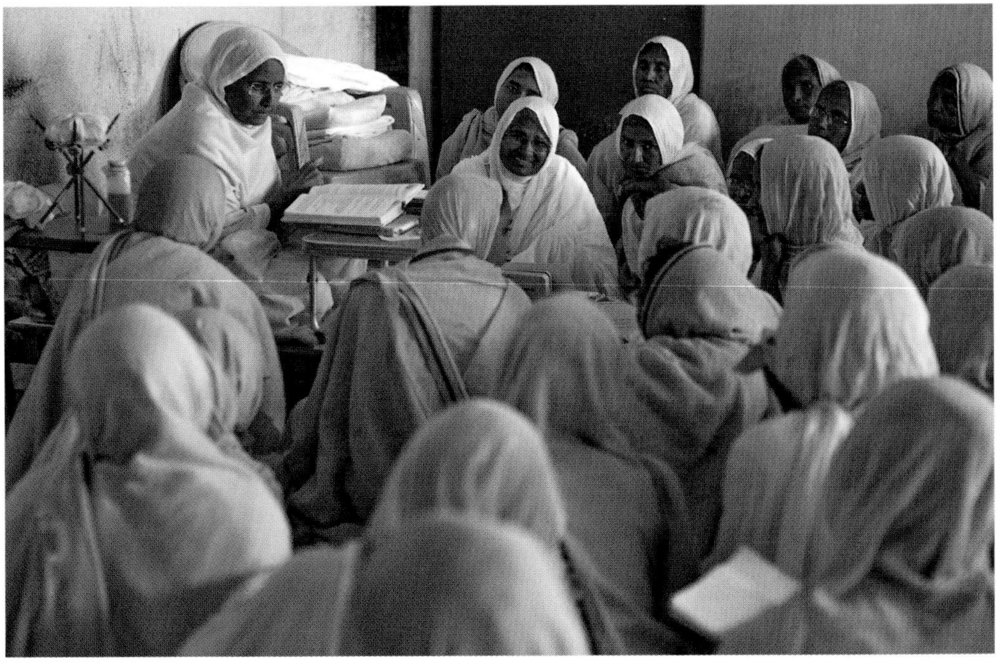

Swetamber Jains' daily discourse with Pujya Shri Prashmitashriji Maharaj Saheb,
Uttar Pradesh, 2016

PAGES 78–79
Swetamber Jain nuns sorting through and distributing the last possessions of a nun,
Kolkata, 2015

PAGES 80–81
Swetamber Jain nuns walking to a morning discourse,
Kolkata, 2015

PAGES 82–83 and PAGES 86–87
Acharya Vijay Kirtiyashsuriswarji Maharaj, a renowned authority on Jain Yoga,
Uttar Pradesh, 2016

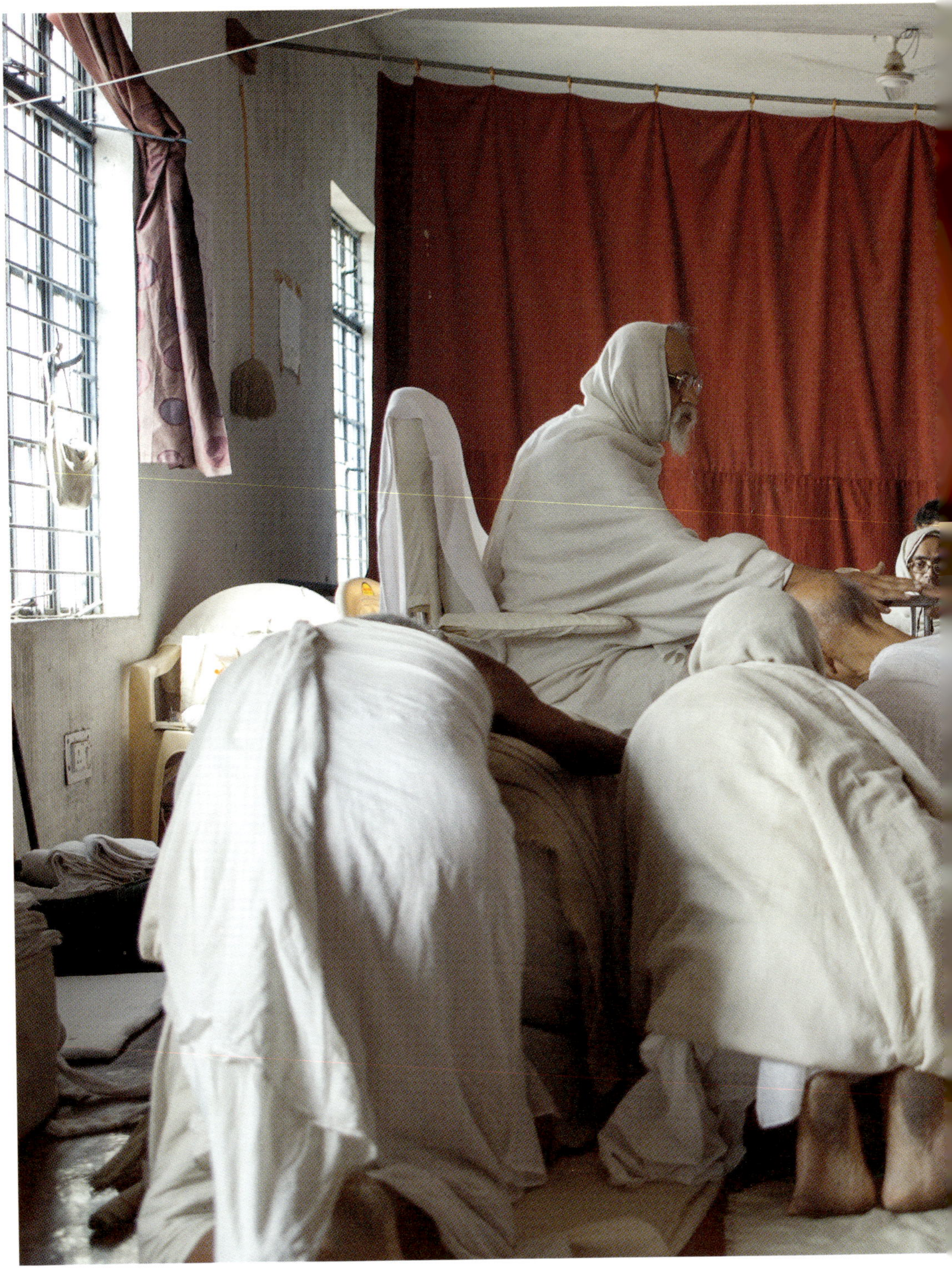

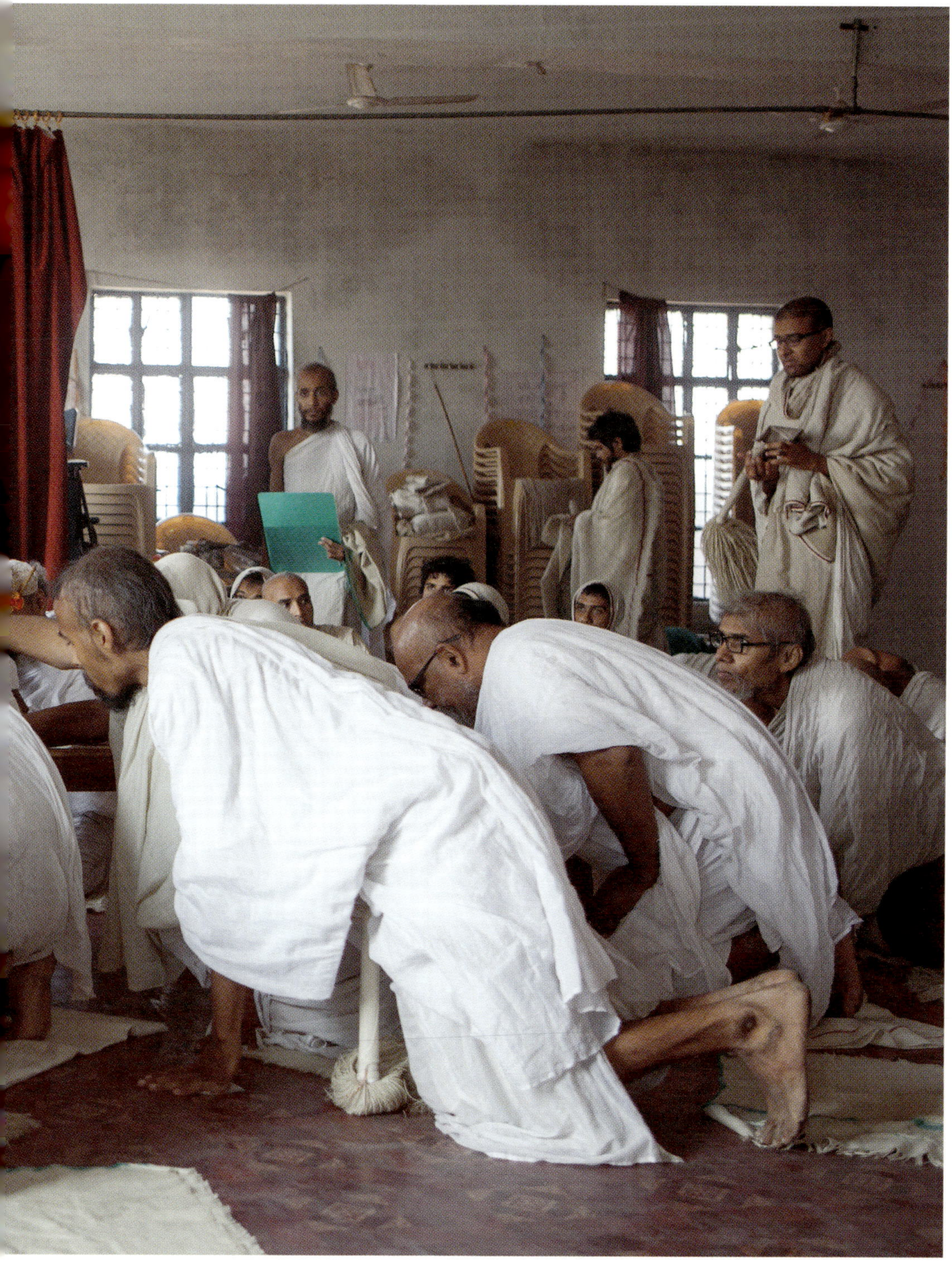

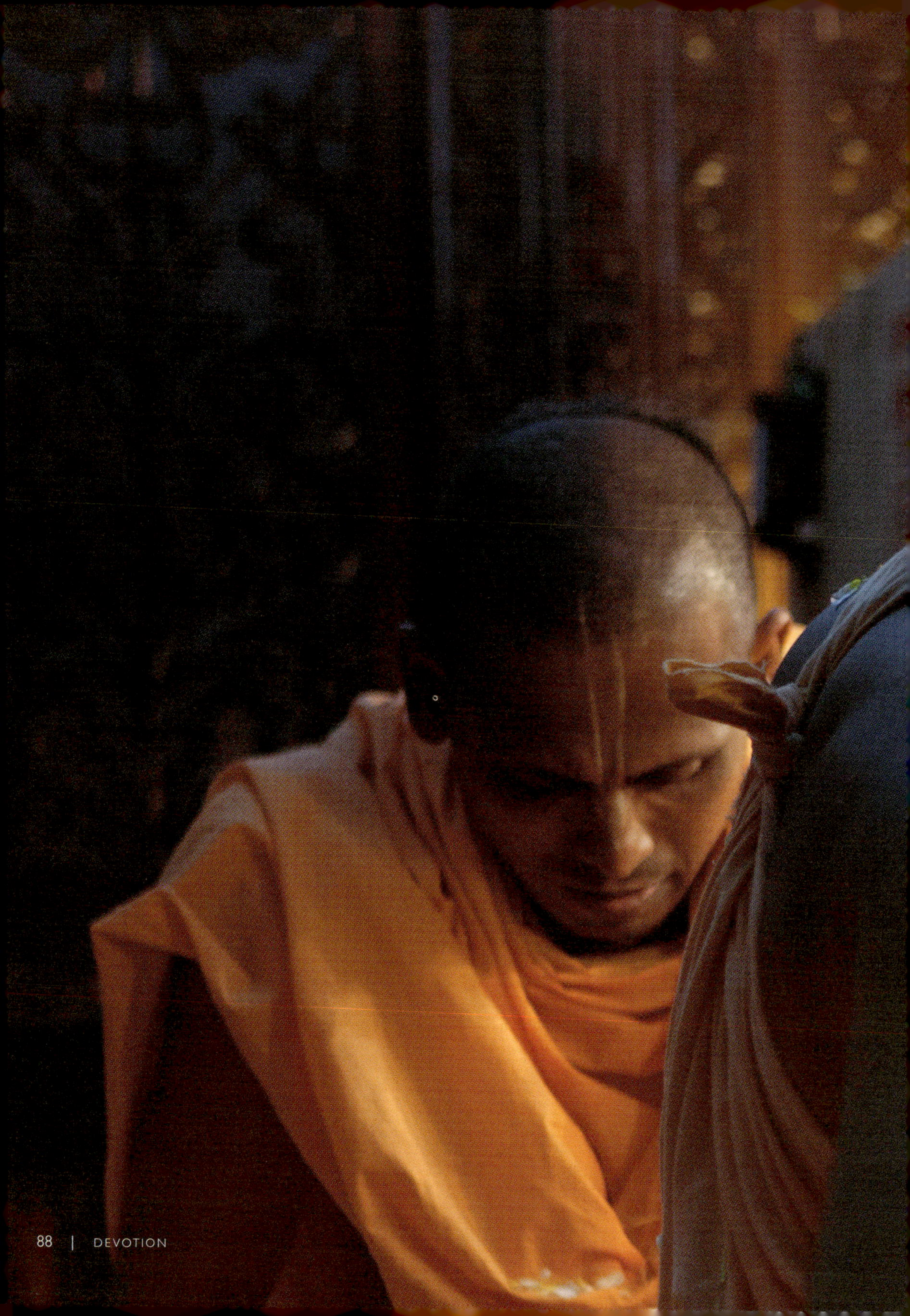

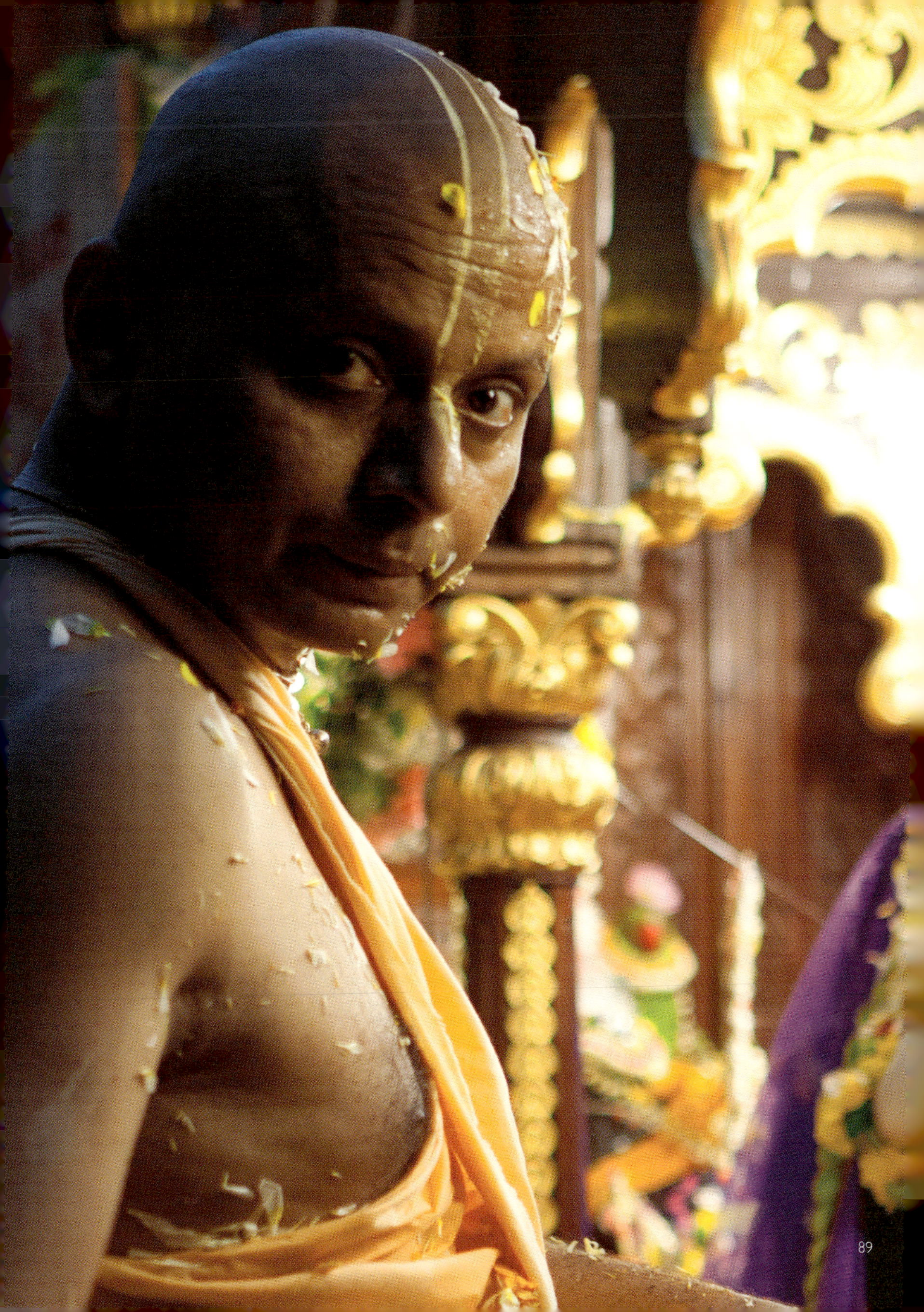

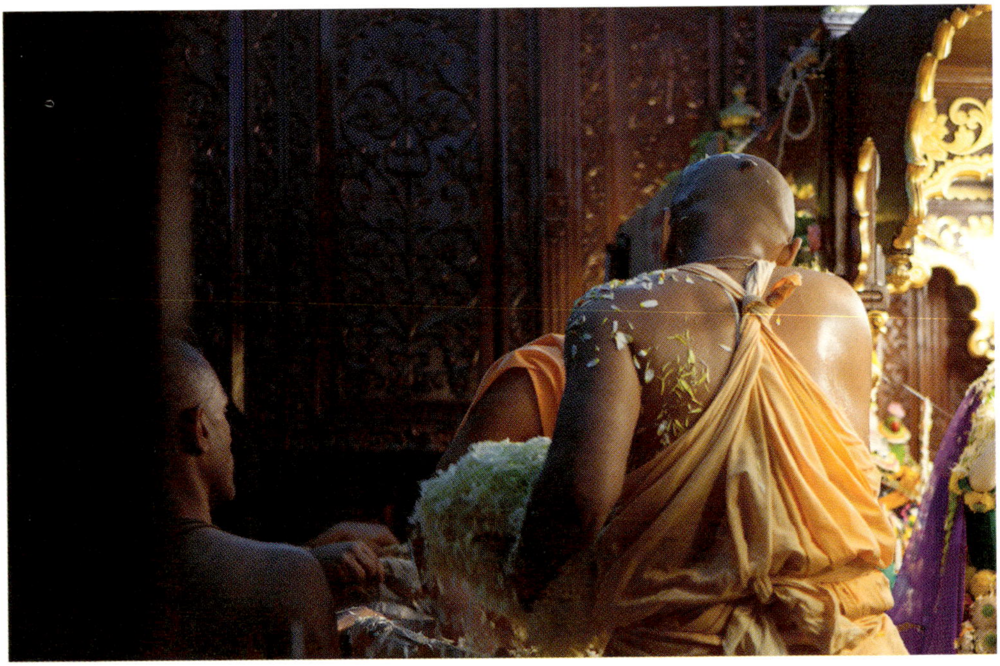

PAGES 88–93

Flower Festival, ISKCON Temple, Sri Radha Gopinath Mandir, Mumbai, 2016

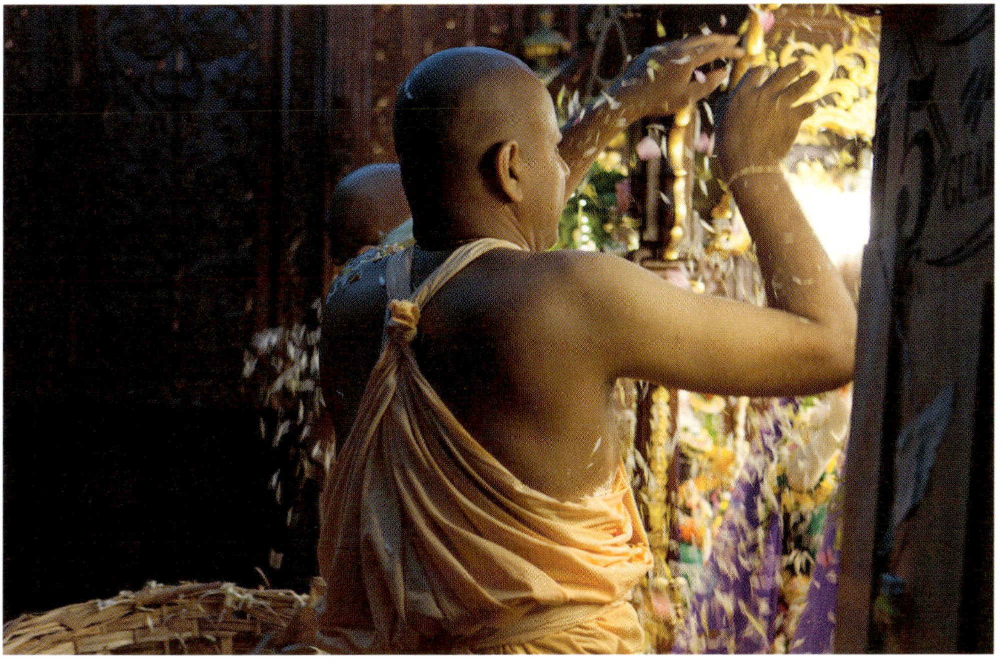

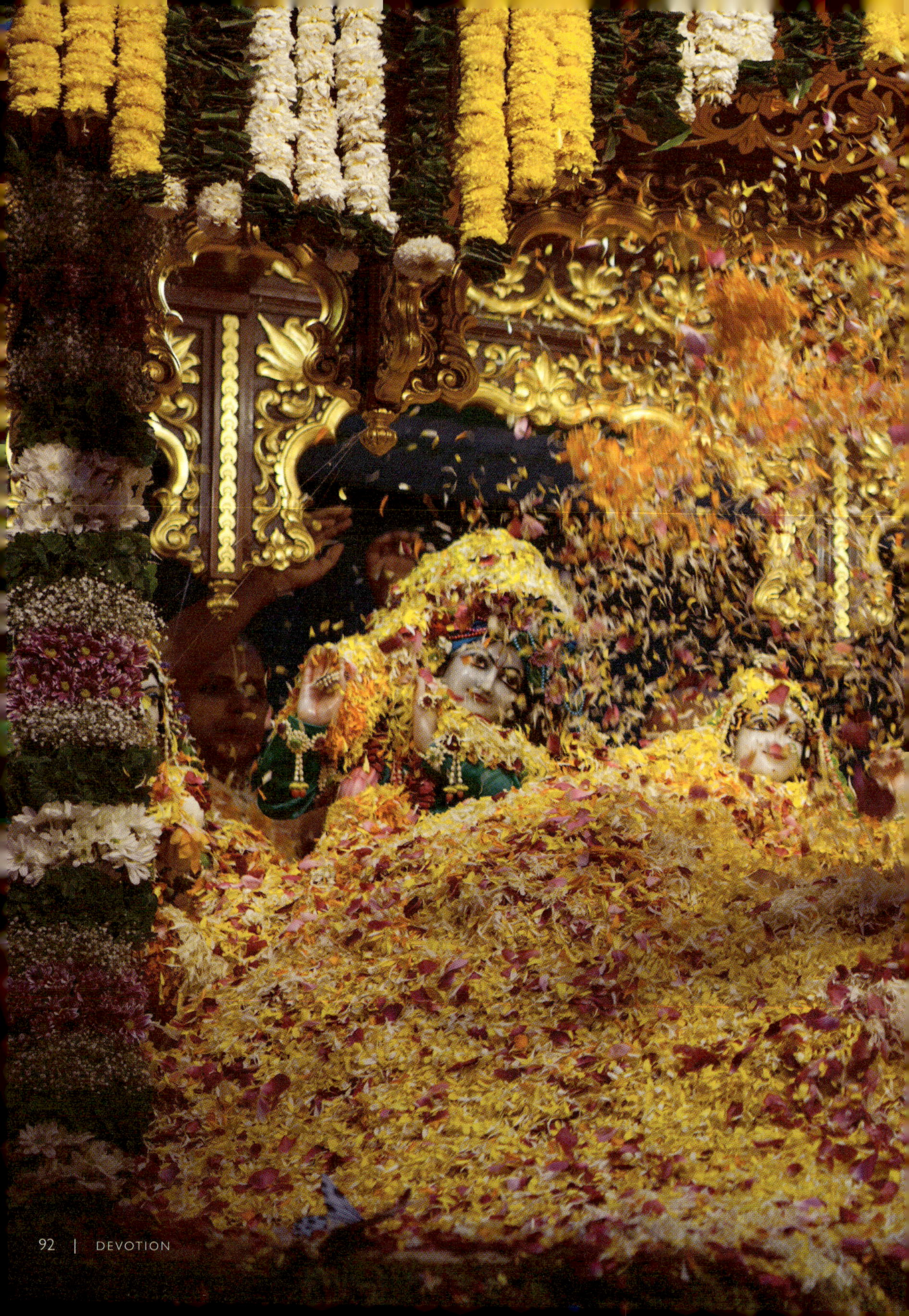

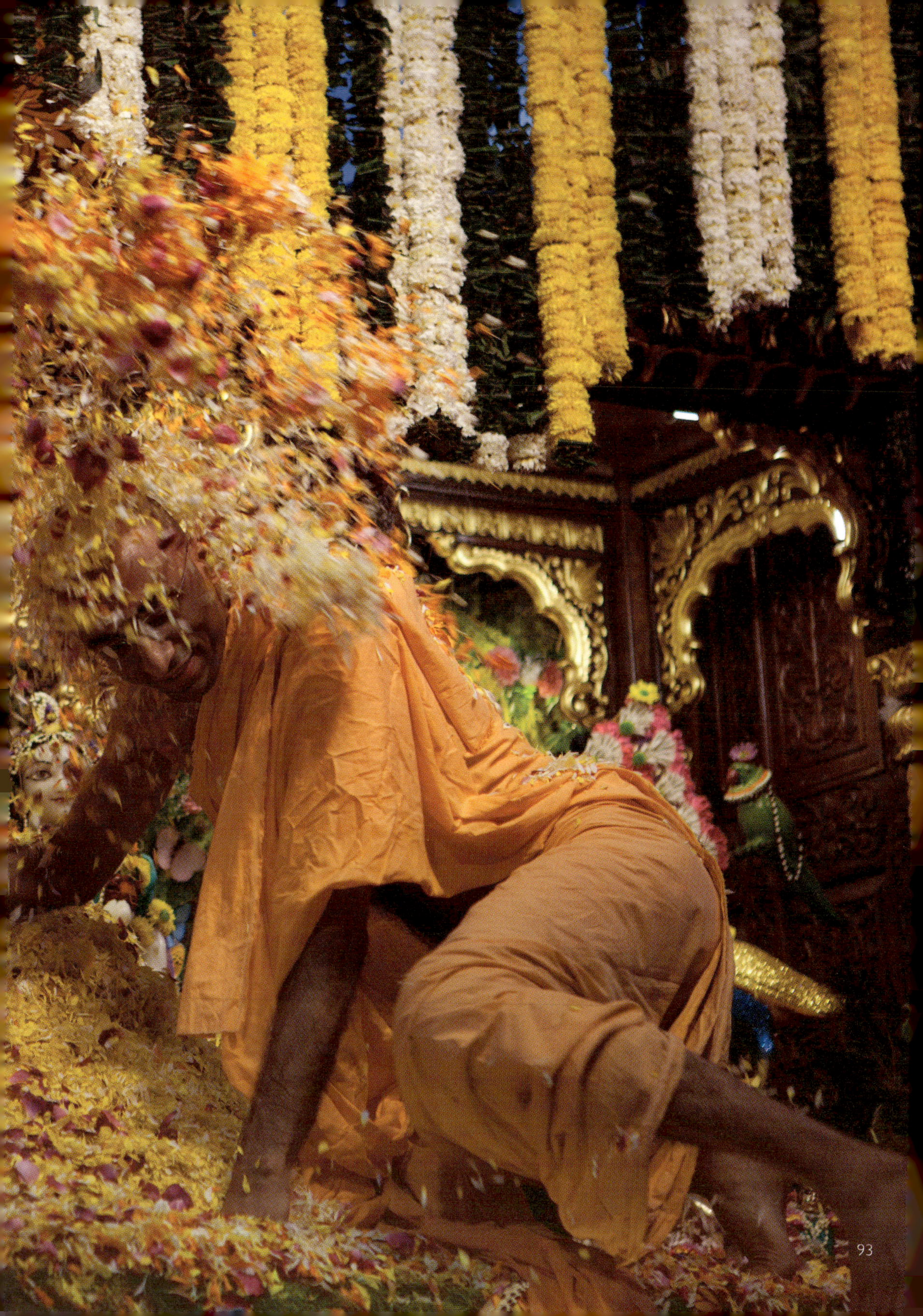

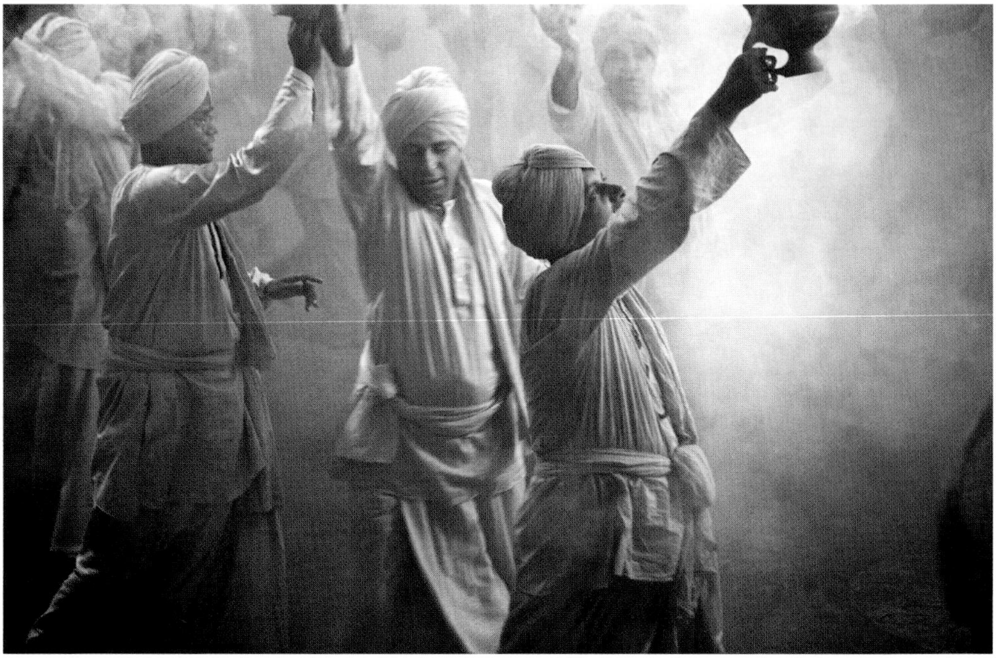

PAGES 94–97

Bharat Sevashram Sangha monks singing and dancing while performing aarti, Durga Puja, Varanasi, 2008

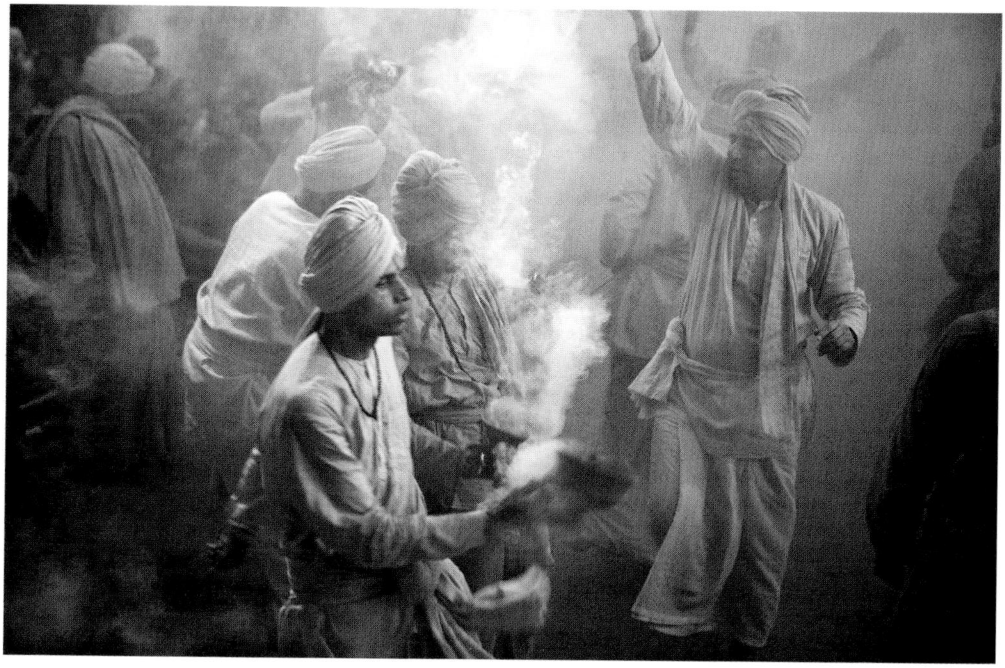

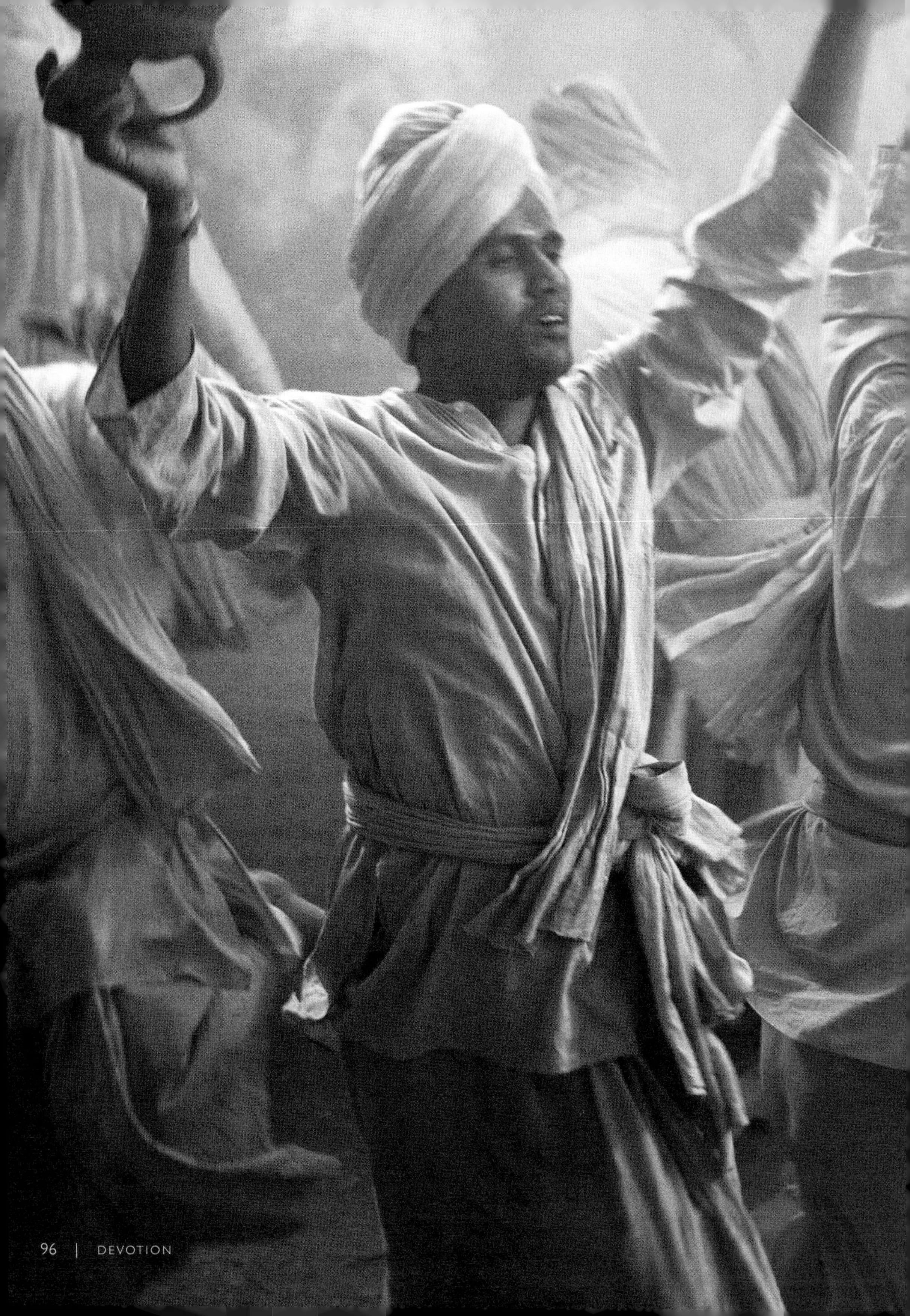

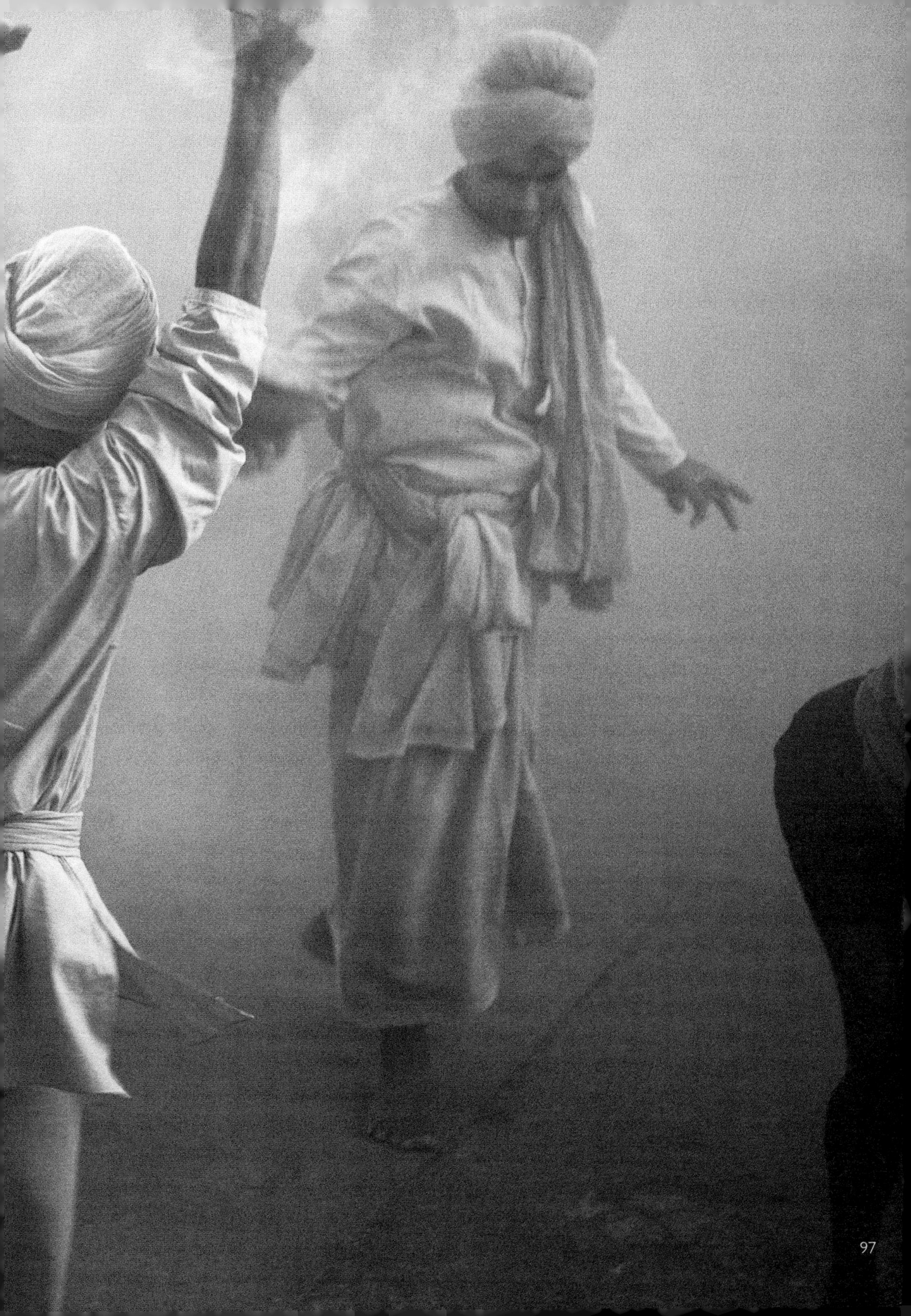

TRANSMISSION

When a candle is lit, and in turn lights another, so too it is said that when wisdom is passed from the guru to the disciple, the transmission is perfect and complete. With no difference now between the two, beauty is fully expressed.

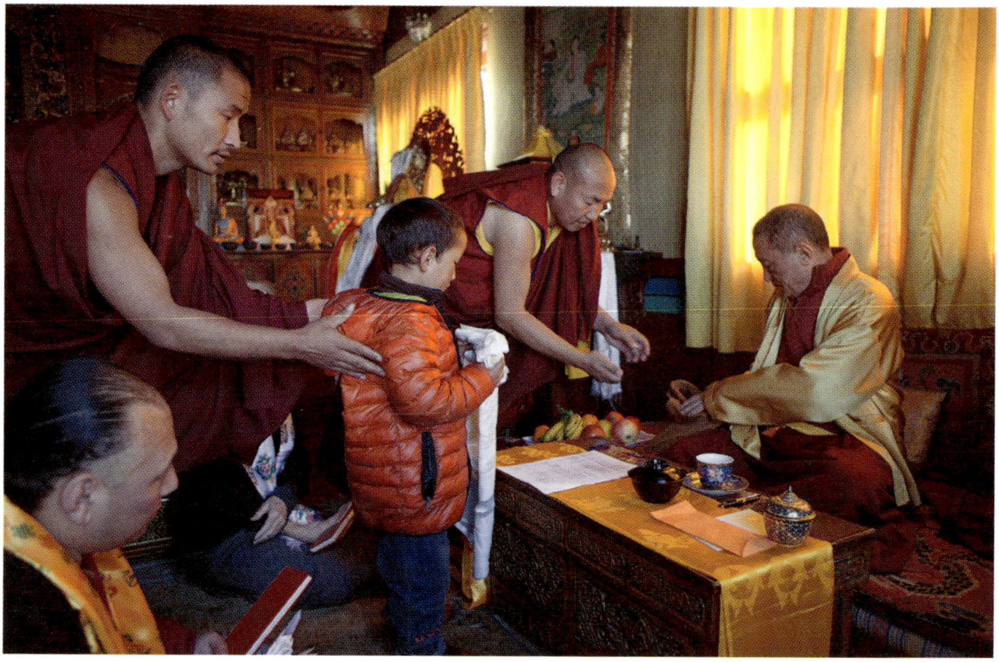

Chokyi Nyima Rinpoche with a young boy offering a khata, a traditional Tibetan scarf, upon his initiation into monkhood, Ka-Nying Shedrub Ling, Kathmandu, Nepal, 2015

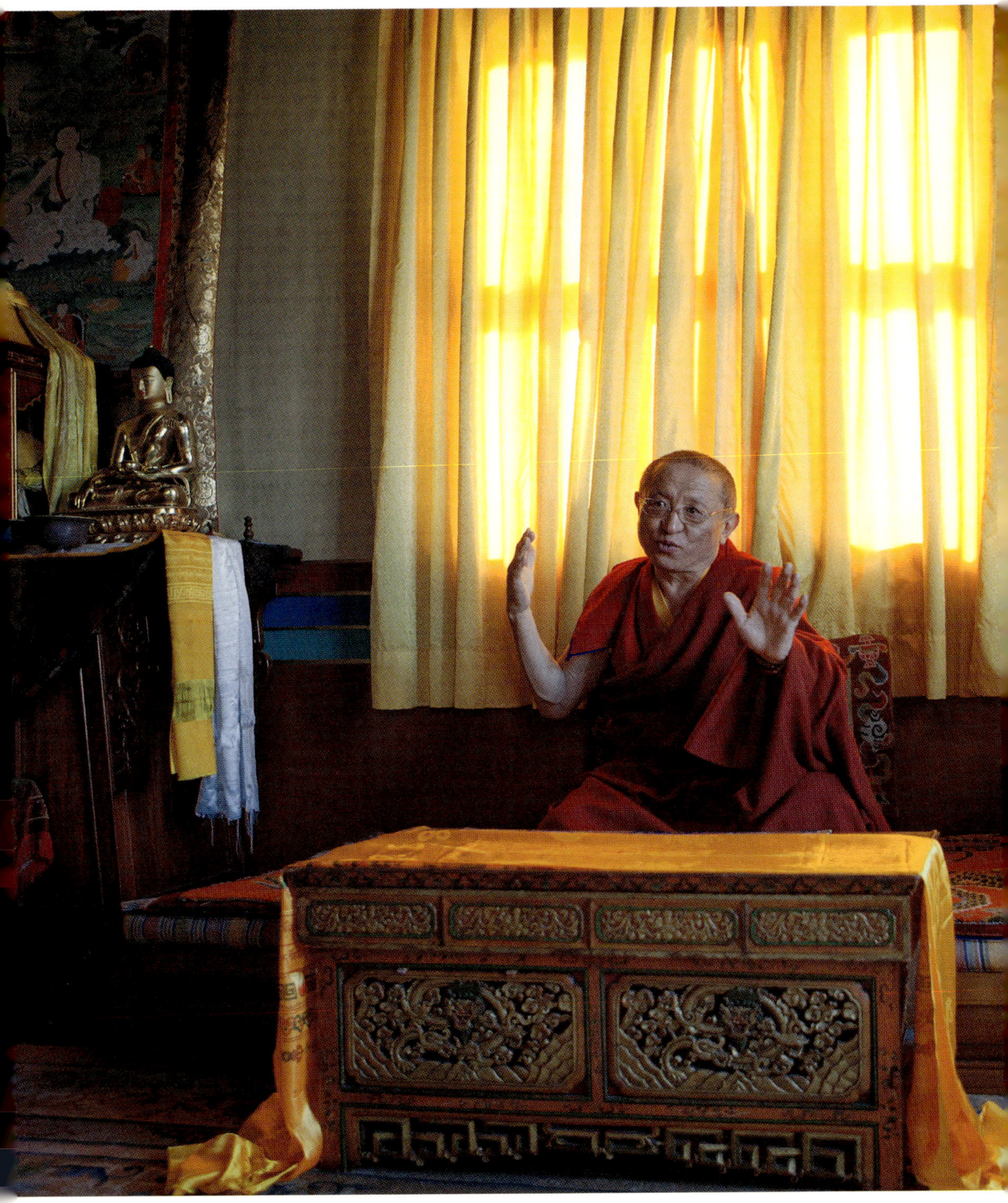

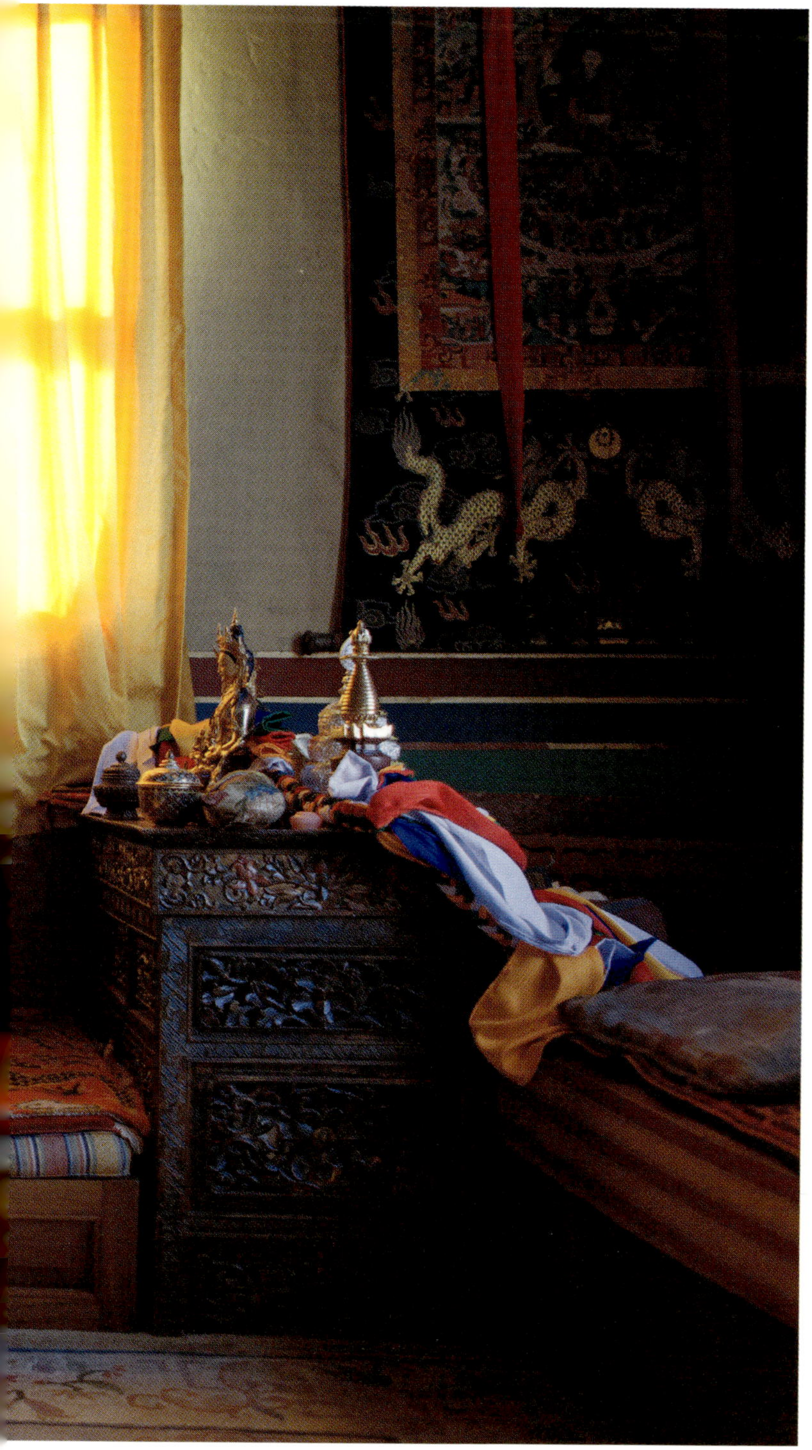

Chokyi Nyima Rinpoche, recognized at age eighteen months as the seventh incarnation of the Tibetan meditation master Gar Drubchen. Rinpoche oversees the welfare and spiritual education of hundreds of monks and nuns.
Ka-Nying Shedrub Ling, Kathmandu, Nepal, 2015

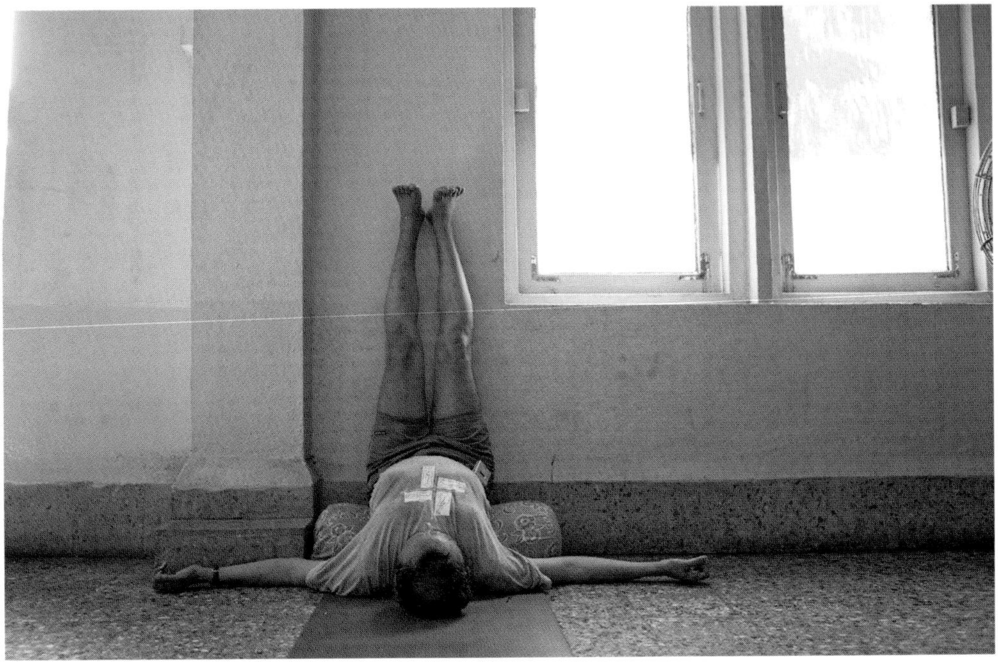

PAGE 104 and 107

Fr Joseph H. Pereira practising Iyengar Yoga, Church of Our Lady of Mount Carmel, Mumbai, 2015

PAGE 105

Fr Joseph H. Pereira performing the rites of the Holy Communion. Ordained a priest in 1967, his Iyengar Yoga practice began ten years later – opening up a new dimension to his spiritual pursuit.

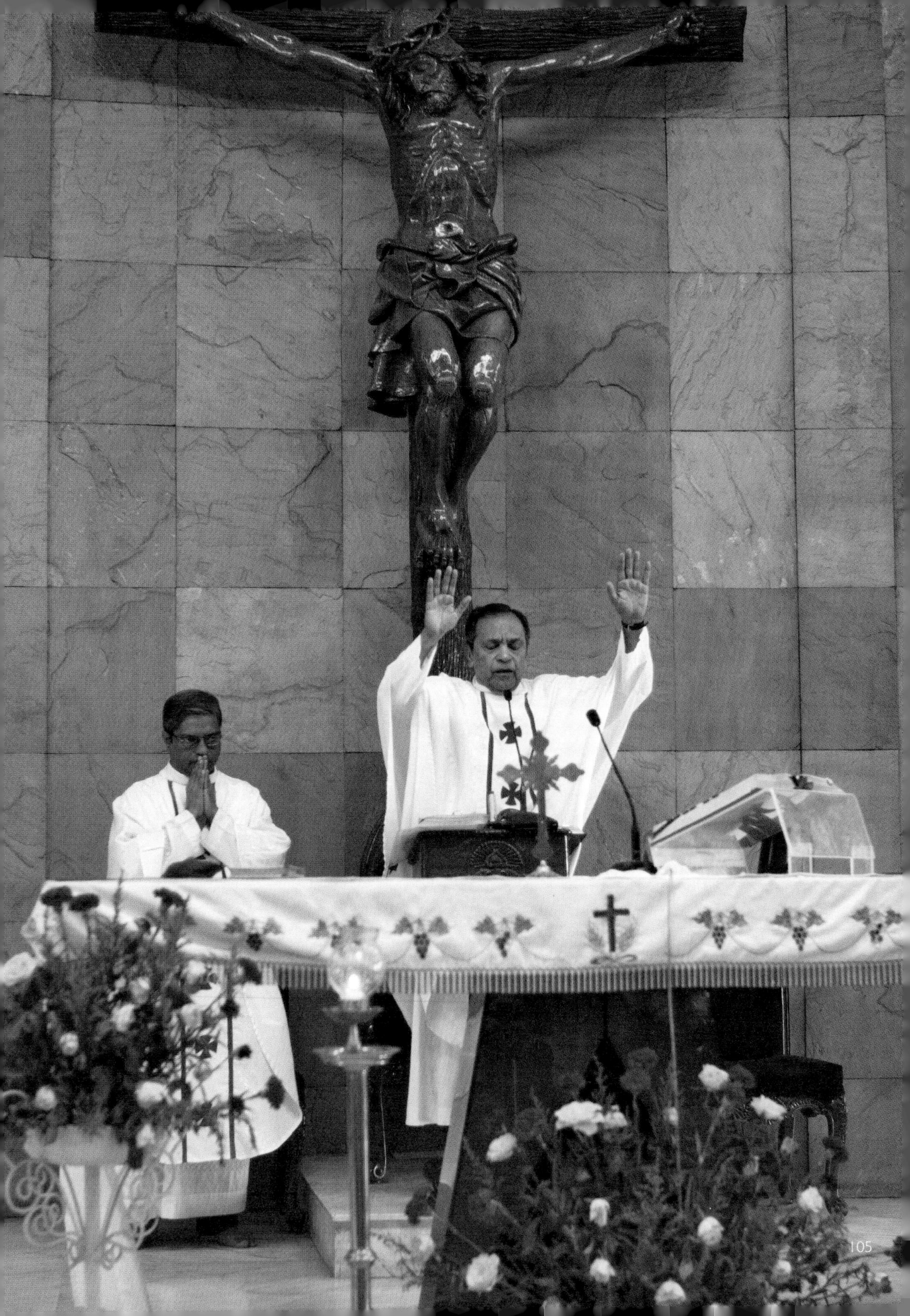

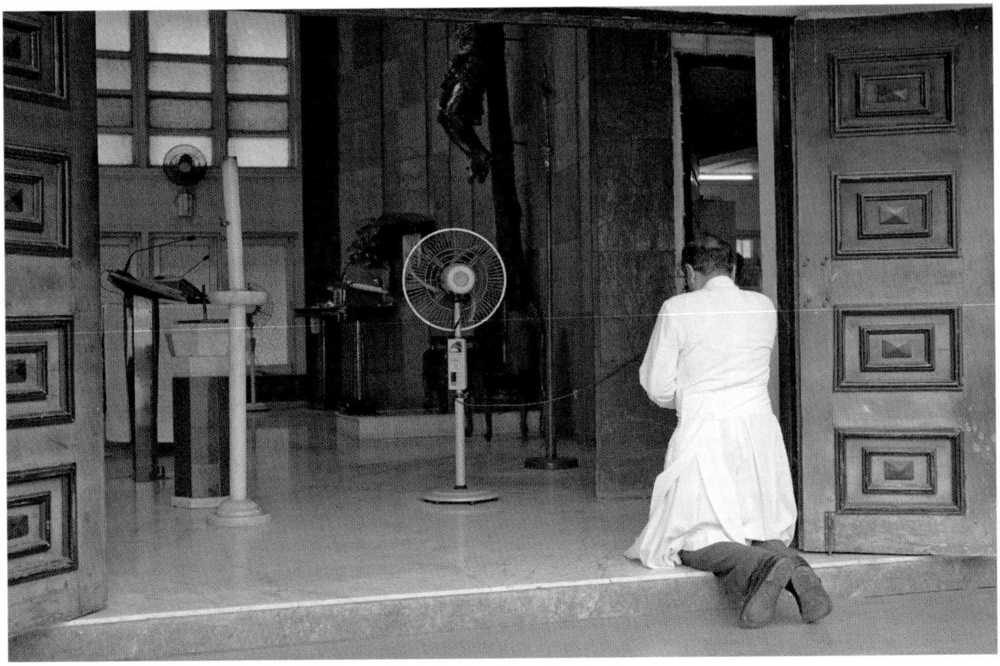

Fr Joseph H. Pereira in prayer,
Church of Our Lady of Mount Carmel,
Mumbai, 2015

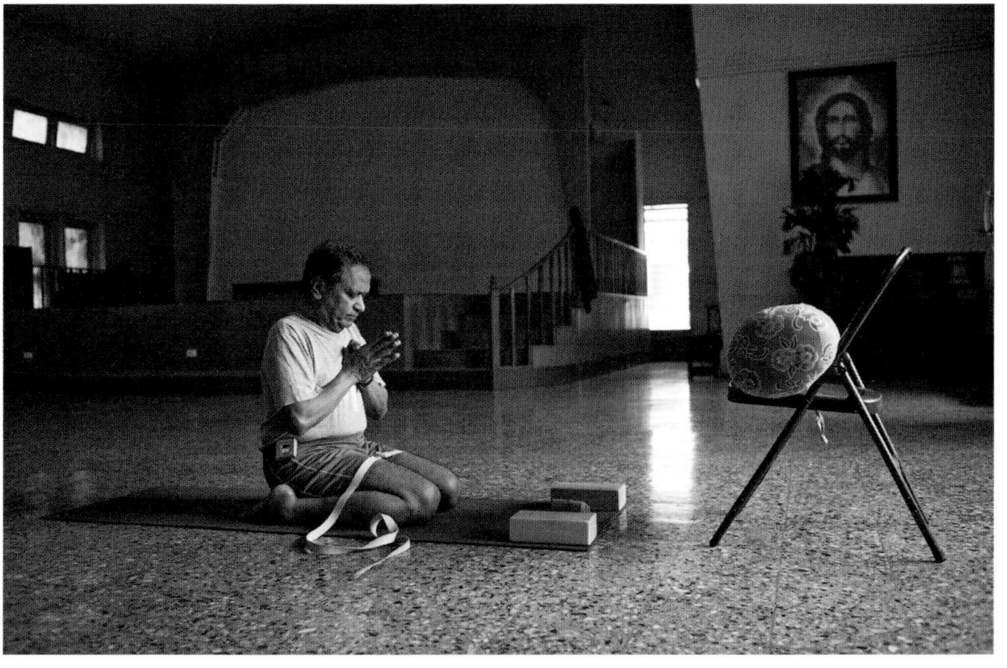

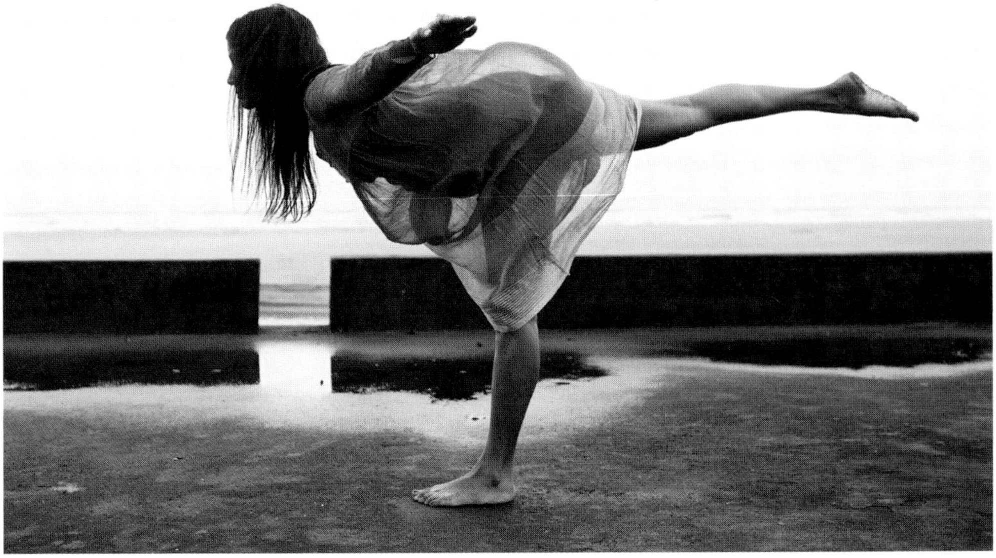

Sharmila Desai practising Ashtanga Yoga,
Ashvem Beach, 2015

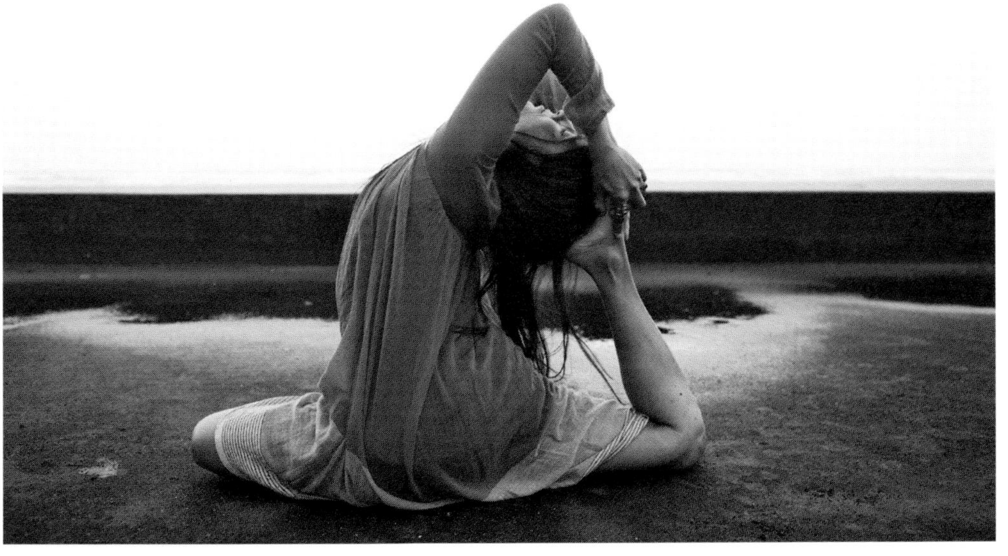

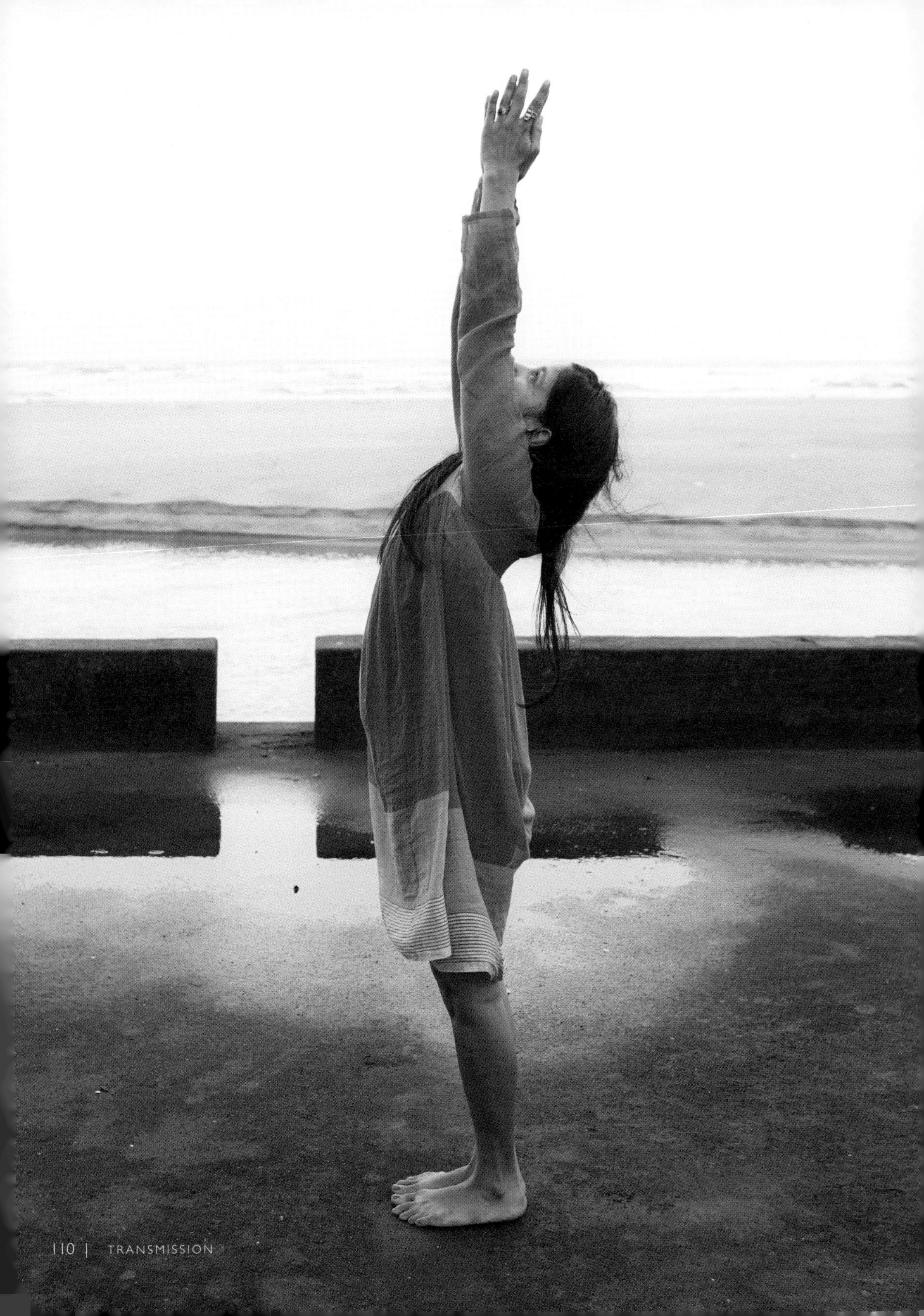

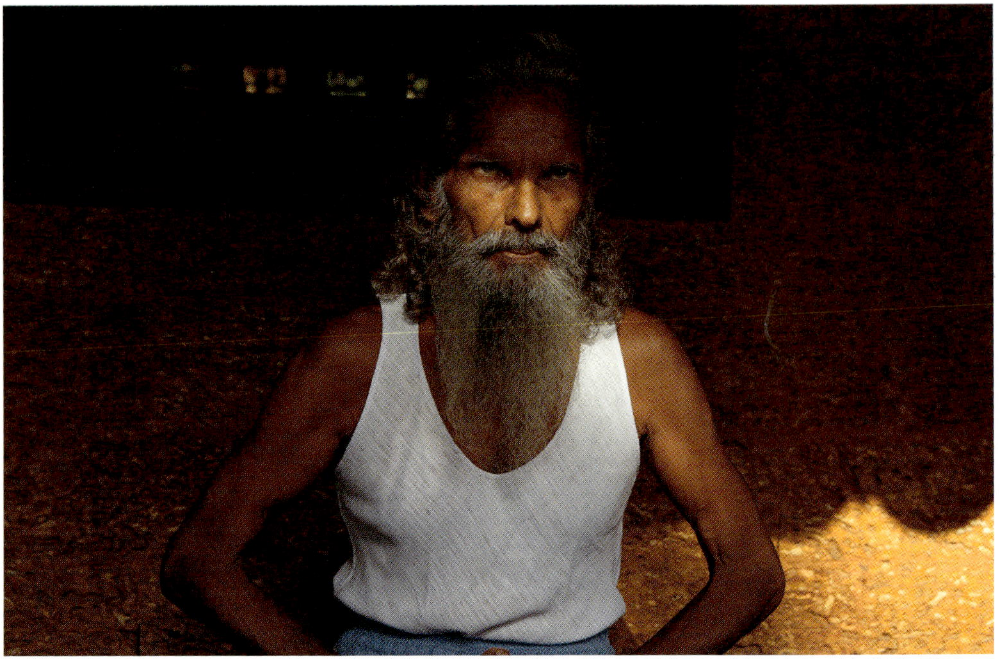

K.V. Krishnan in meditation,
Hindustan Kalari Sangam, Calicut, 2014

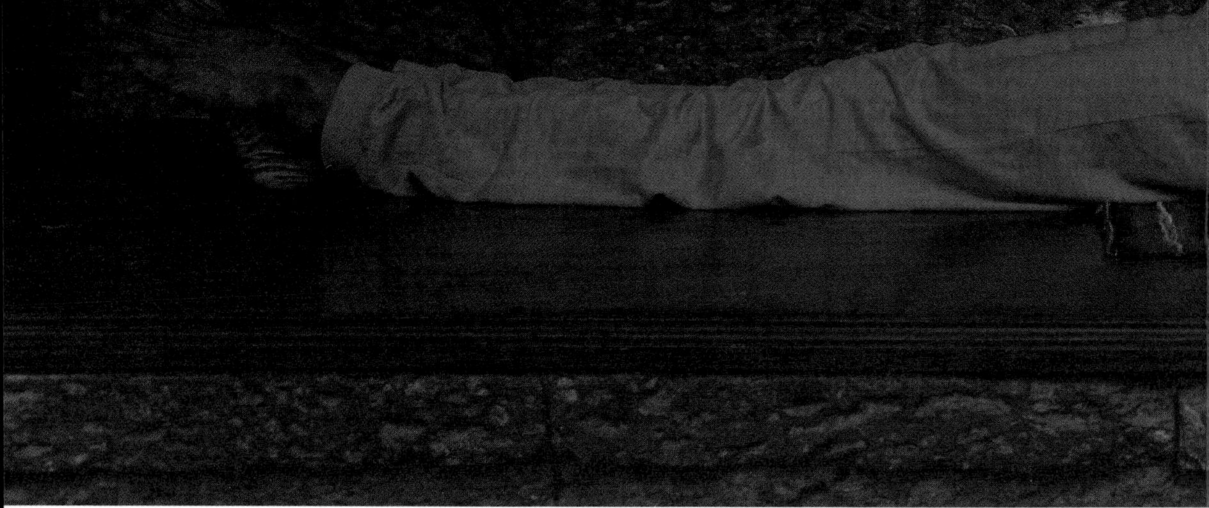

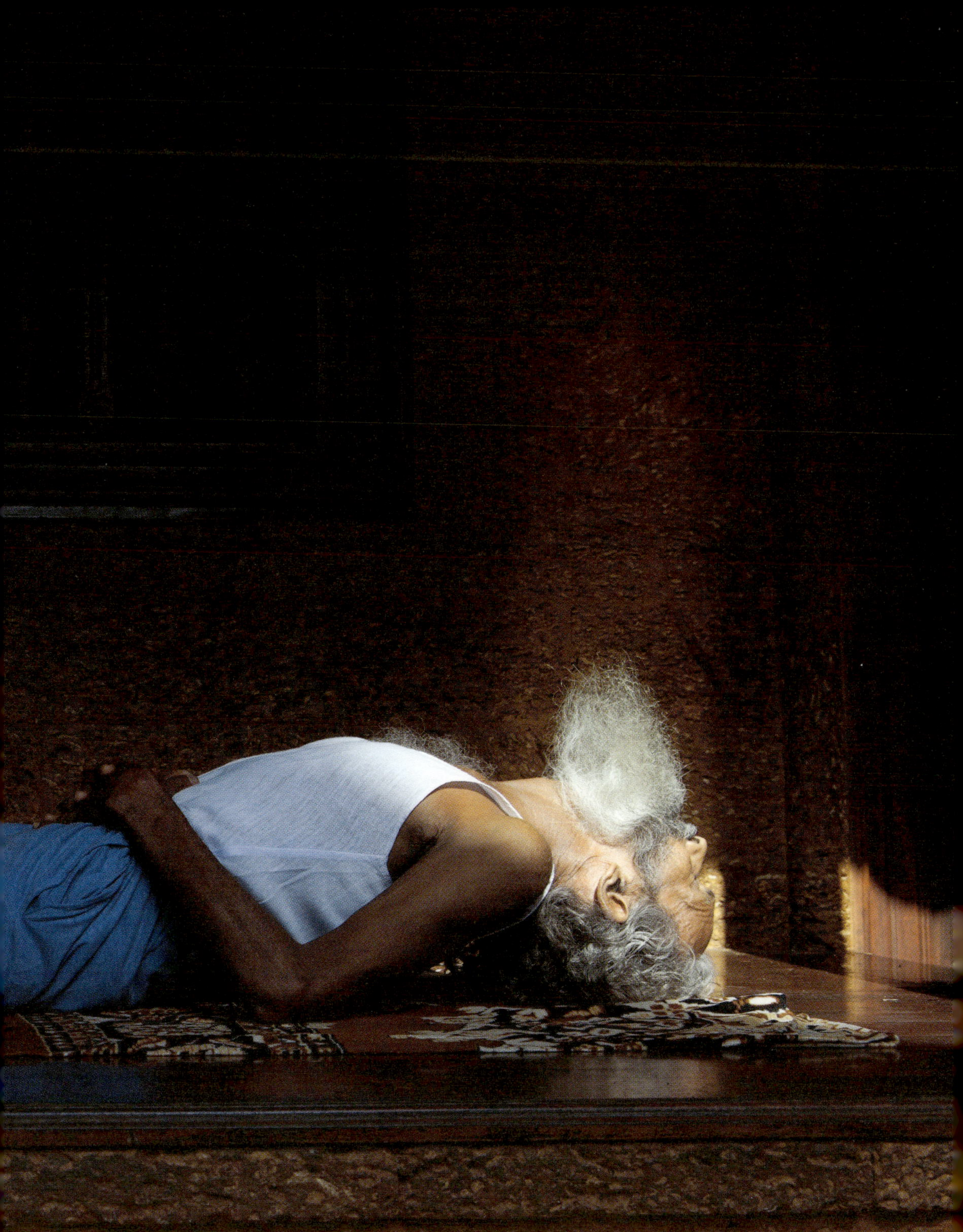

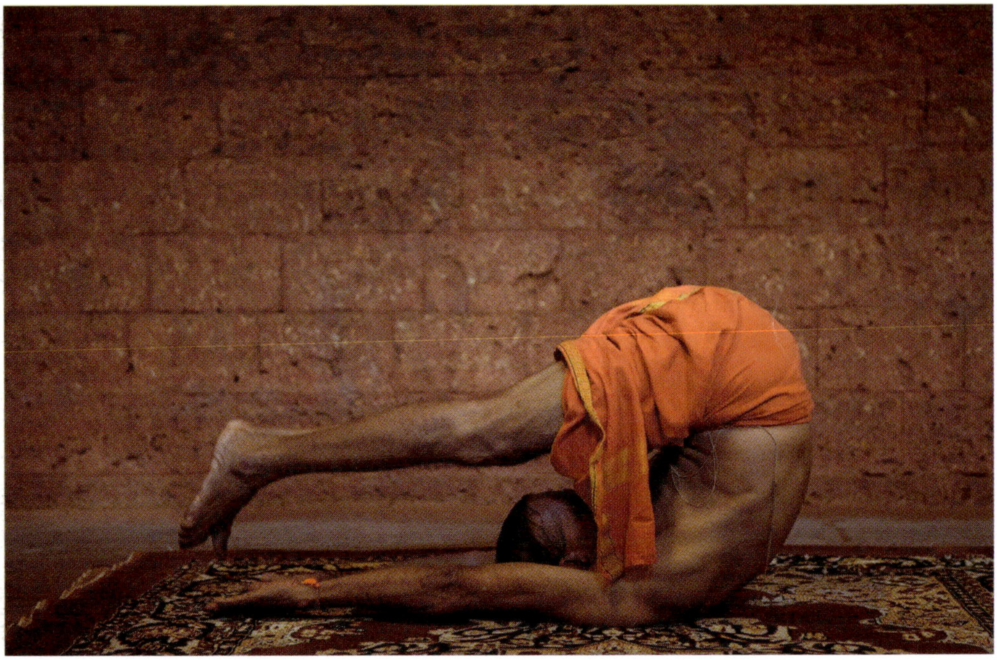

Yogacharya Padmanabhan practising
Ashtanga and Tantric Yoga,
Hindustan Kalari Sangam, Calicut, 2014

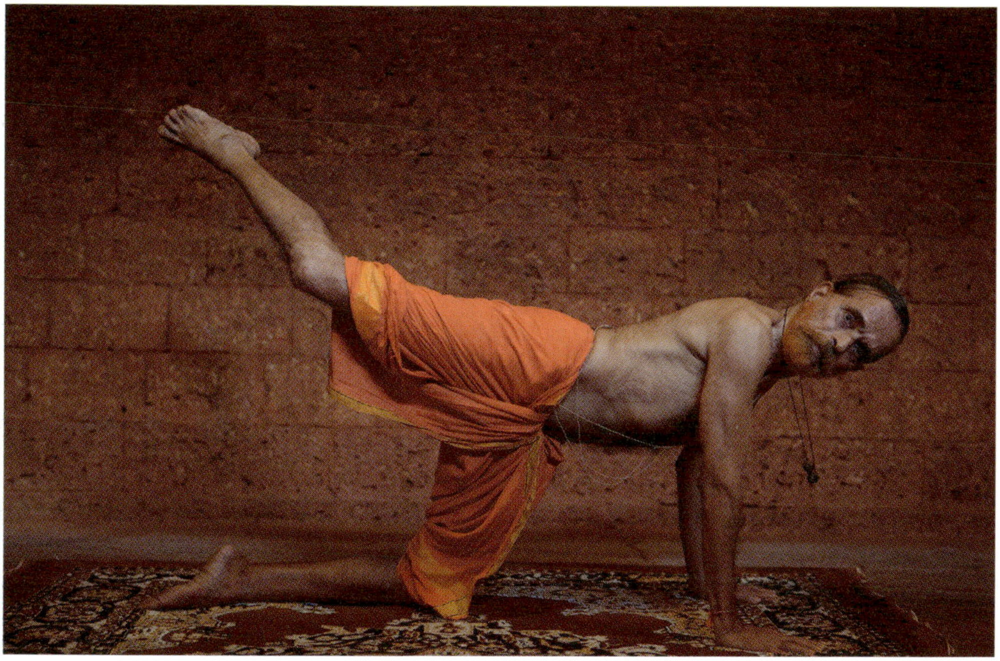

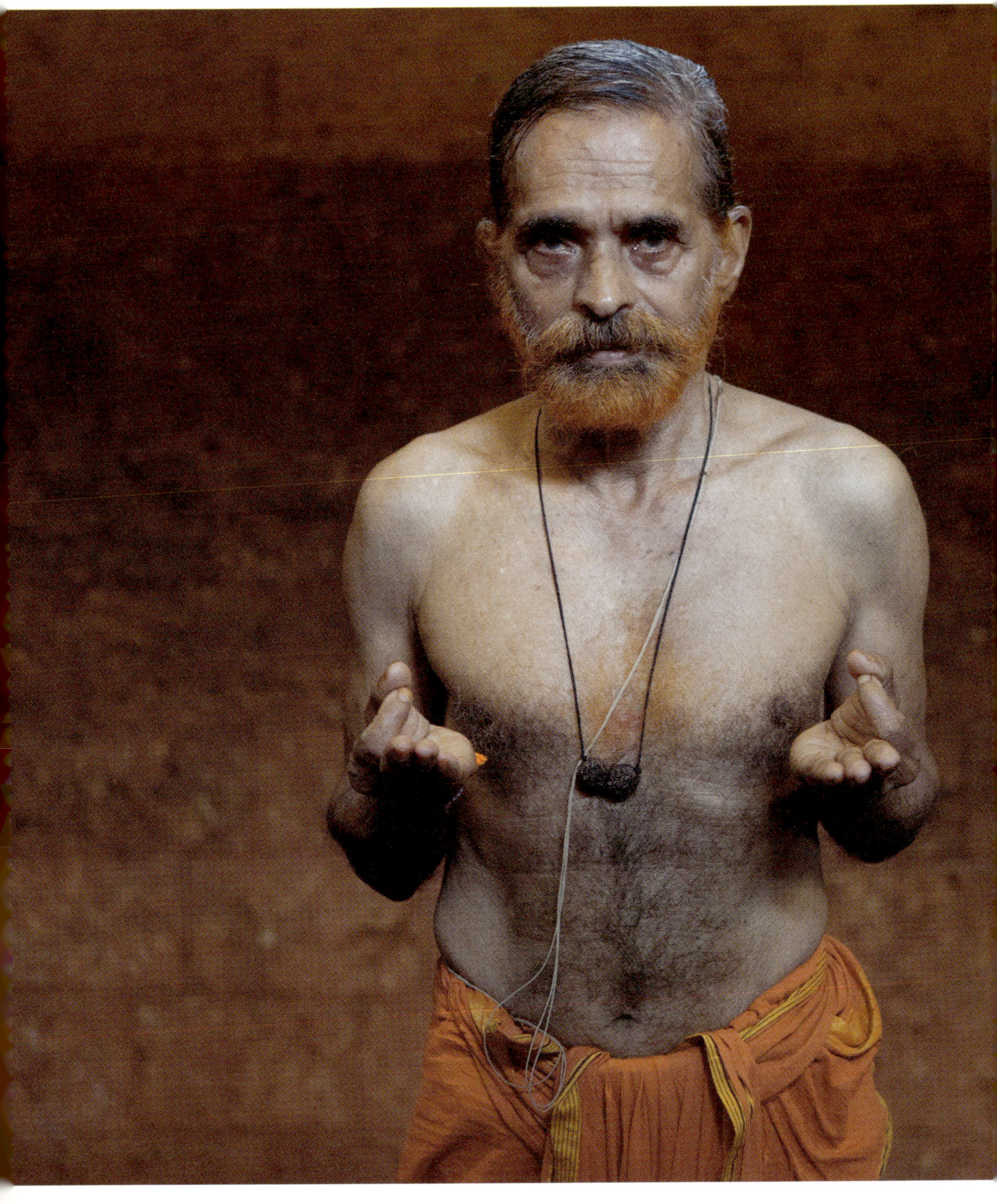

Yogacharya Padmanabhan,
Hindustan Kalari Sangam,
Calicut, 2014

PAGES 120–121
Acharya Vijay Kirtiyashsuriswarji Maharaj,
Swetamber Jain Monastic Order,
Kolkata, 2015

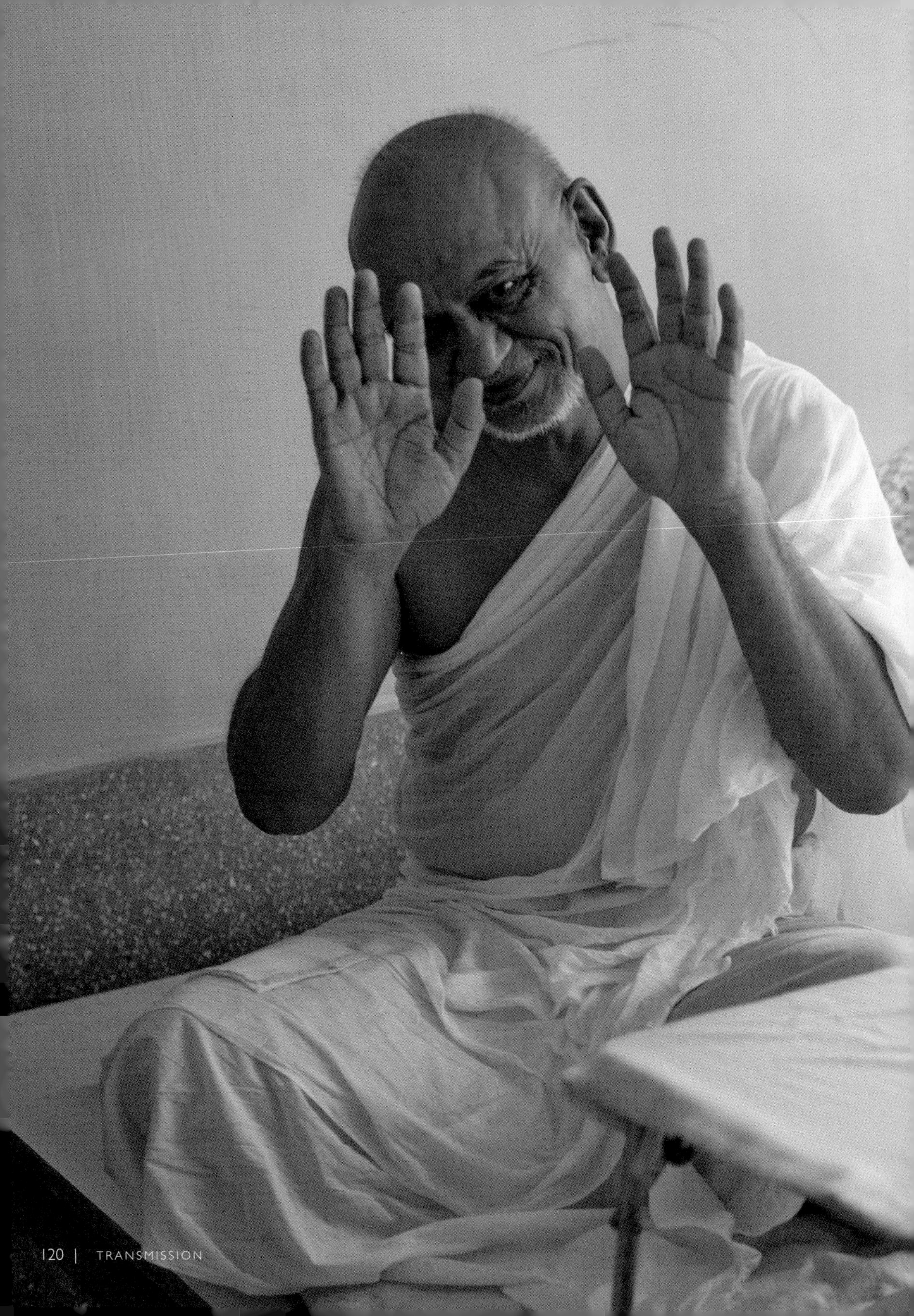

APPENDIX A

Acknowledgements

There are many extraordinary souls I met on the path who wished to remain anonymous. They graciously agreed to share their knowledge and they all remain in my heart.

To Tsering Gellek for sharing her wisdom and being the guiding force behind this book-making journey. Words cannot express my deep gratitude.

Thank you to all those who generously contributed to the production of the book: Melissa and Ralston Roberts, Annalisa Albini, Spiros Antonopoulos, Michael Fisher, Philip Andelman, Craig and Candace Anderson, Betsy Barnett, Ipsita Sarkar, Ranjeev Bhatia, Nikhil Khera, Akshat Bhatt, Emily Allen, Freyan Billimoria, Ann Ernish, Laurence Bornet Fayol, Sabrina Buell, Ruth Westoby, Ben Carson, Fiona Caulfield, Libby Kacich, Radha Chadha, Brett Davis Collins, Loriann Fall, Kenneth Fong, Zachary Gisterak, Cassy Gleason, Lauren Godfrey, Kaisa Kinnunen, Unni Krishnan Karunakara, Leah Kinsella, Natalia Lauricella, Sam Miller, Molly Ney, Jennifer Newman, Rymn Massand, Arthur KcKeown, Diana Oberlander and Nomad Chic, Amy Priya Santos, Akila Seshasayee, Charles Pignal, Usha Prajapati, Carla Provenzano, Monique Romeiko, Maya Seely, Jofree Shimray, Barry Silver, Megan Marissa Steinman, Rajat Sodhi, Olivia Tincani, Amanda Walker. Kiran Rao & Amethyst, William Bissell, Anne Gorrissen, Amy Carol Smith Ainscough and Somak Ghoshal for the in-kind support we received.

To Justin Peters' commitment to the vision of this work and designing these pages. This book would not have been made without you! To Mike Racz for retouching and Chris Cantley for stepping in at the end for the final push. So grateful to you guys!

With gratitude to Dzongsar Jamyang Khyentse Rinpoche, Prashant Varma, Tashi Coleman, Amit Dasgupta, Dr Anita Dudhane, Niranjan Gogia, Sachin Dante, Chelna Shah Jain, Reuben Abraham, Radhika Singh, Lina Krishnan, Anup Shai, Rajesh Thomas, Hindustan Kalari, Dr Lal, Niranjan Gogia, Tejbal Pandey, Mr Chandrasekaran, Mani Iyer, Rajni George, Tripta, Sanjib Chatterjee, Shivani Goel, Sarover Zaidi, Aparna Nadiem, Malti, Vishnupriya and her beloved teacher Bhagavan, Uma Prajapati Haimavati, Rhea Zimmerman, Catherine Meukens, Samir Saran, Regan Williams, V. Sunil, Sylvia Rascon, Ronnie Cziska and Yogini for walking with me on the path.

Ratna Raman and Rimli Borooah for their beautiful words, and to our very patient editors Marina Bang and Shyama Warner.

To all those I photographed and researched with who shared their precious time and contribution: Acharya Vijay Kirtiyashsuriswarji Maharaj, Pujya Shri Prashmitashriji Maharaj Saheb,

Muni Samvegayash Vijay Maharaj, Sadhvi Jinpragnyashri, The nuns and monks of the Swetamber Jain Monastic Order, Ashtanga Yoga Student at International Chandramauli Charitable Trust, Lucy Guest, Charlotte Leech, Anuska Ilijic, Sage Berry, Lourdes Perez, Khampagar Monastery, Tokdens at Tashi Jong, Maulana Jalaluddin Abdul Mateen, Shah Syed Hasnain Baqai, Mohd Jamin Qureshi and Reshma Qureshi, Siraj Khan, Jetsunma Tenzin Palmo, Gelong Kalsang Tenzin, Tersi Osal Dorje Rinpoche, Sarnath International Nyingma Institute, H.H. Chatral Rinpoche and Saraswati, Pema Gellek and Lama Palzang, Doshu Lama, ISKCON Chowpatty, Radhanath Swami, Kaustubha Das, Radha-Kunda Das, Avtarlila, Bharat Sevashram Sangha monks, Punam Chopra, Lama Thinley, Jigmet Norbu, Lama Shatup Raphel Rinpoche, Tashi Rabgias, Ani Tsultim Wangmo, Ani Tenzin Dolma, Chokyi Nyima Rinpoche, Fr Joseph H. Pereira, K.V. Krishnan, Yogacharya Padmanabhan, Ananda Panda, Ramakrishna Math, Sharmila Desai, Ajmer Sharif Dargah, Peerzada Anwar Rahman Jilani, Shia Cleric Kalbe Jawad, Swami Muktananda, Surendra, Swami Hariomanand, Swami Janardhanananda, Yogananda Ashram Kolkata, Ravi Shankar, Swami Govindananda, Bihar School of Yoga and Swami Niranjananda, Gautam and Gopa Sen, Swami Nitaya Muktananda, Rajeswari Ranganathan, Sudhin Ray, Shree Bidyut, Swami Suddhananda Giri, Swami Viragananda, Sewaram, Pooja Ratnakar, Rummy, Dheeraj Banta, Swami Govindananda, Shiju T., Kailaimani Shanmugananda, Robert Moses, Dr Sampad Mishra, Gita Kumar Pandit, Manoj Pavitran, Orgyen Tobgyal Rinpoche, Yogi Saji, Hemant Kumar Tiwari, Swami Vigyananda Giri, Vishnu Sunil, Vijay and Ali Khan and Mata Amritanandamayi Devi.

To my beloved teachers over the years – Betsy Barnett, Eddie Stern, Therese Poulsen, Jamanagiri Swami and the lineage of Sri K. Pattabhi Jois, I am ever grateful to your guidance.

My thanks to HarperCollins India: Ananth Padmanabhan, Rakesh Chander, Shantanu Ray Chaudhuri and to dear Bonita Shimray for believing in my work.

With gratitude to the Vadehra Art Gallery and Vidya Shivadas for their commitment to my photography.

Pico Iyer for his generous and kind introduction. Thank you for opening your heart to this work.

And to my dear friends who have taught me so much about loving and living in the moment, everyday.

I love you all.

APPENDIX B

Contributors

Pico Iyer is the author of many books, among them, most recently, *The Art of Stillness*, *The Man Within My Head* (about Graham Greene) and *The Open Road*, a book-long meditation on the first thirty-four years he spent talking and travelling with the XIVth Dalai Lama.

Tsering Palmo Gellek was born in California to Tibetan Lama Tarthang Tulku and beloved Nazli Nour. She lives between Sonoma, California, and Sarnath, India, and is the director of the Sarnath International Nyingma Institute.

Ratna Raman is engaged with language, literature, cooking and travel in the waking hours of her life. She teaches at a Delhi University college and has a column in *The Tribune* (Chandigarh) called 'Mind Your Language'.

Shyama Warner is a freelance editor with over thirty years of experience in editing fiction and non-fiction. She has worked on both *Dance of the Weave* and *Within Without*.

Vishnupriya (*Karie Ann North*) grew up in California and is now based at Satyachetana Ashram in Tamil Nadu, India, where she serves the Satyachetana International Spiritual Movement.

Justin Peters is a New York City-based designer and creative director with over twenty-five years of experience of working with top-tier consumer brands, professional services companies, non-profit organizations and governments around the globe. Justin's travels and encounters have inspired him to push his design thinking beyond commercial applications, and seek out opportunities to empower underserved communities, support creative communities and bring hidden, human truths into the light. *Within Without* is Justin's second collaboration with Briana Blasko, and yet another proud moment in his pursuit of deep and compelling projects and partnerships that move people beyond their everyday.